NUMINOSITY

NUMINOSITY

Photographs, Paintings & Text by

RICHARD LOUIS PERRI

numen | noun | the spirit or divine power presiding over a thing or place. ORIGIN early 17th cent.: from Latin.

REGENT PRESS
Berkeley, California

Paperback
ISBN 13: 978-1-58790-432-5
ISBN 10: 1-58790-432-2

Hardback
ISBN 13: 978-1-58790-433-2
ISBN 10: 1-58790-433-0

E-Book
ISBN 13: 978-1-58790-434-9
ISBN 10: 1-58790-434-9

Library of Congress Control Number: 2018936899

Printed in the U.S.A.
REGENTPRESS
Berkeley, California
www.regentpress.net

DEDICATION

To Dr. Sterling Bunnell, MD
for
his
words,
wit,
wonder
&
wisdom

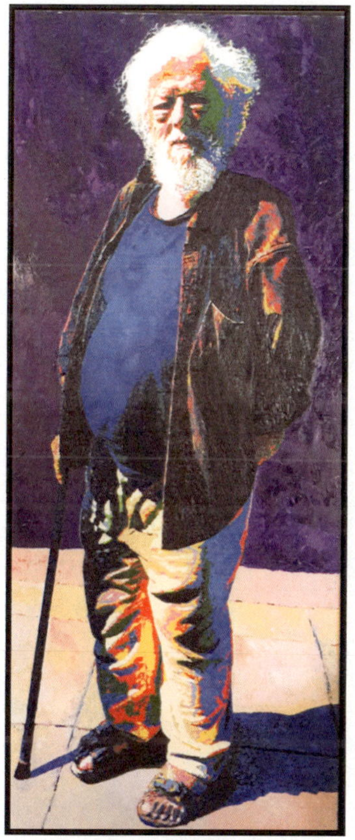

STERLING STANDING
oil on canvas 40"x 96"

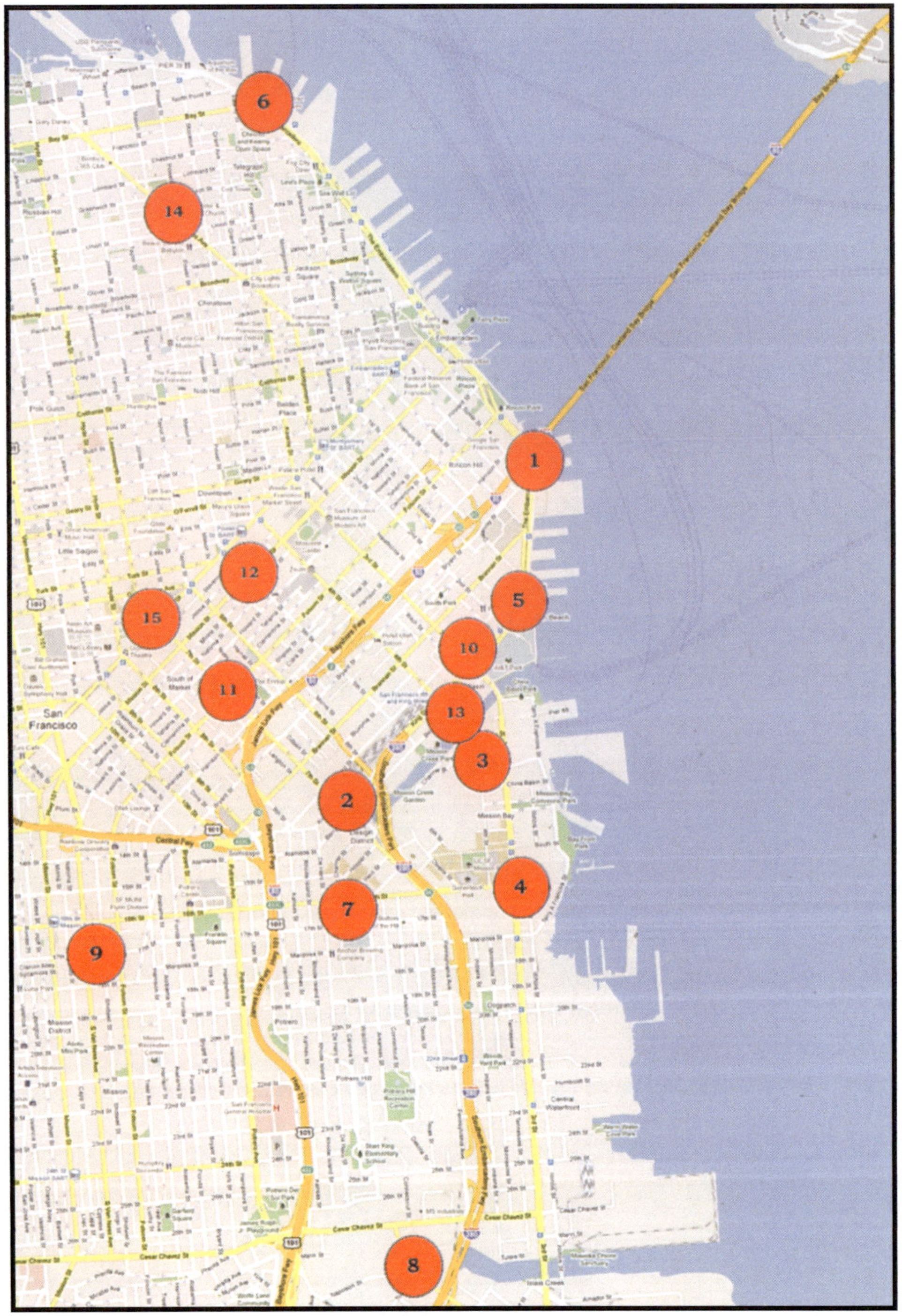

MAP LOCATIONS

CONTENTS

AUTHOR'S STATEMENT

Your hands are holding a book that tells a story about a unique and remarkable view of San Francisco.

Of all the wonderful things people find in this city, there are special places that emanate its strength and character. These are the iconic cafés and diners scattered along the waterfront and industrial side of town known as Java Huts and a couple of other significant places and things. Their special stature and historic influence is remarkable and emblematic of the numinosity they embody.

In this book you see my paintings of the Java Huts done from 1995 to 2005. Next to them are my photographs of what they look like now. Though many locations look much like they did in my paintings, some have changed and others are gone.

No matter what happened to them, these vanishing historic landmarks are immortalized in this book, my paintings and in the minds and memories of those who see them. The Java Huts have numinosity carrying the message of a bygone era and a spirit of the infinite past.

— Richard Louis Perri, 2018

FOREWORD

San Francisco is pretty classy these days, shops selling caviar in the Ferry Building, upscale restaurants on the waterfront, bars that offer three kinds of martinis.

Richard Perri remembers a different San Francisco, a place where the waterfront was full of working men, tough guys, whose idea of an evening cocktail was a shot and a beer after work.

The city—and the waterfront in particular—was full of small coffee joints, where the coffee was strong and black and a cheeseburger was haute cuisine.

A different city, Perri remembers, easy to get around, tough to dislike. Parts of the waterfront were shabby and run down and you had to be careful at night, watch your step. It could be rough, but it was as real as a ten cent baloney sandwich.

Perri started painting this San Francisco just before it vanished. He hung out in places where you washed down a hamburger with a Budweiser, and the literary life consisted of reading the Sporting Green. He visited junk yards full of old streetcars, and streets lined with rusty railroad tracks.

The city was changing and everybody knew it. The ships were going to Oakland, and along with them the old warehouses, the drayage companies, and the men who worked there. So he painted this world.

This book is a sampling of what he saw. San Francisco only yesterday.

— Carl Nolte
San Francisco Chronicle Staff Writer

PREFACE

In many of our minds the images of certain places or dwellings occur in dreams or as backdrop to waking experience. Imbued with subtle yet powerful feelings and meanings, they may represent a more ancient and inclusive way of thinking.

Richard Louis Perri has worked for many years, continually refining his art. Here he has given us an array of diners which have in bygone years been temporary hearths to unknown numbers of workers, artists, and vagrants who gravitated to them. In his paintings we see them in timelessness, ringing with numinosity.

Those of us who were born in San Francisco and have had the good fortune to grow old recall many such places. If there is indeed a universal memory, as some believe, it is by such icons that our city will be remembered

— *Sterling Bunnell, M.D.*

INTRODUCTION

How many ways can one view a city? Countless ways, I should think. We have the memories of those who live in cities, we have literary descriptions, and we have the visual arts — painting, photography, drawings, and such.

As these views stretch out over time, as though some mammoth cinematic panorama were unfolding, we realize that the views, the objective reality of the city, are in a state of constant change as inexorable as Heraclitus' observation, "You cannot step in the same stream twice."

Artist Richard Louis Perri has chosen San Francisco as the city to illuminate the steady architectural transformations that occur in an urban environment. In an idiosyncratic series of images his book *Numinosity* presents a dramatic staging of change.

Most of the images are of eating places. Not the chic or fashionable restaurants that come and go in the modern urban setting, but the eateries of sometimes dubious quality that catered to the workers in the local industries — the stevedores and longshoremen of San Francisco's once-bustling port, the laborers in the food-processing plants, the toilers in the produce district.

In addition, Perri's brush captures other eclectic structures that have caught his imagination — a drawbridge, a church steeple, a federal mint.

Many of these buildings no longer exist, sacrificed on the altar of so-called progress. Others continue on, often in an altered form. The paintings remind us of the fragility of urban reality. Neighborhoods undergo radical contortions. Once thriving businesses disappear. Food tastes undergo a metamorphosis.

But even the establishments that no longer are continue an existence in Perri's paintings. The inviting and vibrant pastel colors and the reassuring geometric quality of the compositions beckon us to think about those vanished structures and about the organic changes that are endemic in a city's history.

Even the buildings that survive tell us of a changed environment. Clientele at the restaurants has no doubt changed. The stevedores and longshoremen are long gone, their places taken by programmers and dot commers, new residents in the gentrified vicinity, and San Franciscans from other neighborhoods who wish for an unusual venue for breakfast or lunch.

Place is an important facet of every person's sense of himself or herself. For the native San Franciscan, a sense of change in his or her urban landscape is both nostalgic and indicative of new opportunities and challenges. For the newcomer place becomes important in sending out new roots. In both his existing body of work and in the work that is to come, Perri celebrates both the sameness and the change of San Francisco.

The photographs that accompany his paintings — one showing an empty lot where once had been a successful restaurant, another showing a recently repainted building that continues to serve an appreciative clientele — add to our sense of loss and our exhilaration at what has been preserved.

Place is an ever-changing dimension. Perri's paintings preserve that which is gone and that which remains.

— ***Professor Charles Fracchia***

Historian, Author, Founder and President Emeritus San Francisco Museum and Historical Society

RED'S JAVA HOUSE

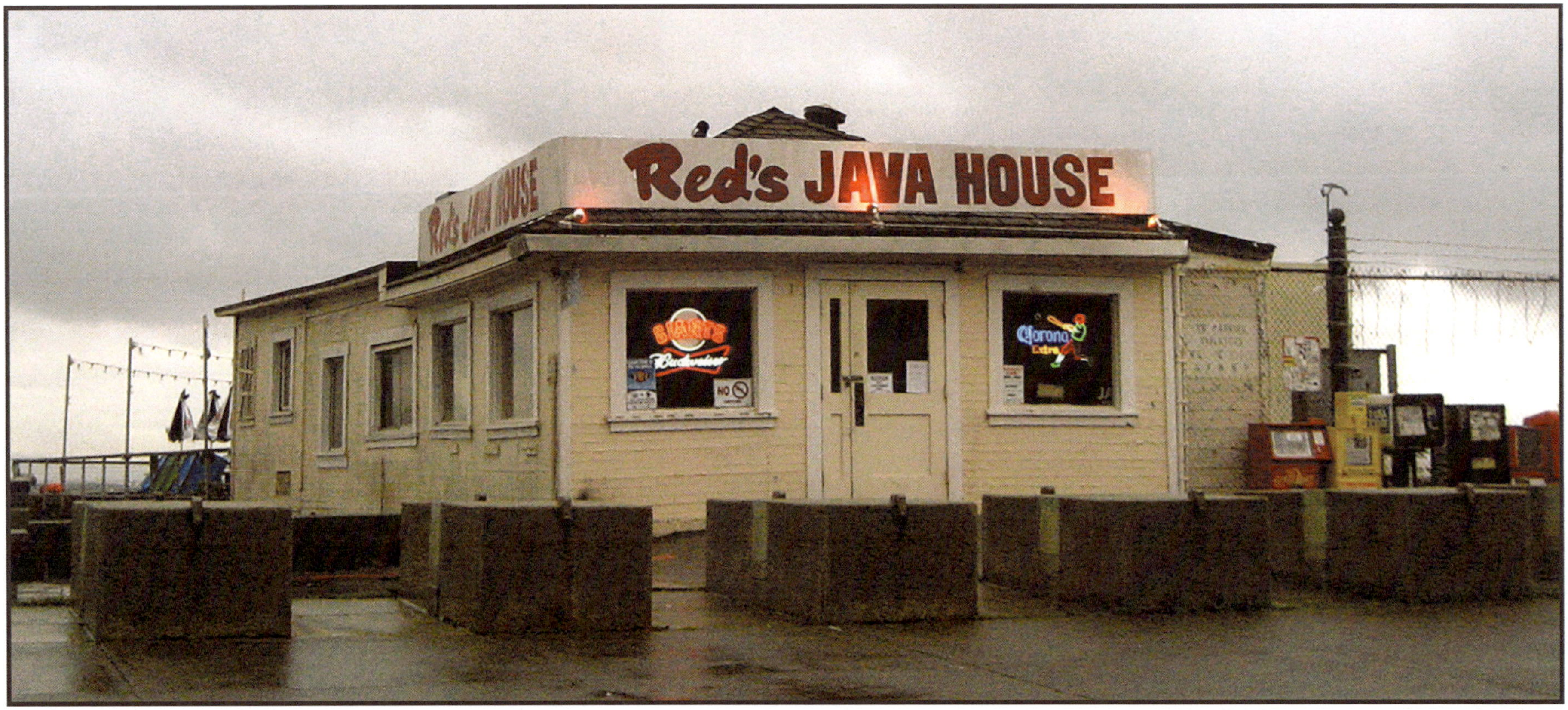

King of the Java Huts

Founded by the once red-headed Tom McGarvey about 60 years ago, this joint, huddled between the long piers reaching out into the San Francisco Bay, served the rough and tumble dockworkers and truckers that shuffled the cargo along the city's port. These longshoremen, the lifeblood of this city, slammed down and fed the city's cargo pallets the same way they slammed down Red's coffee, beer and burgers, feeding their own palates.

Red (Tom McGarvey) loved his Java House and going in to meet all the guys made his day. A real raconteur, he could hold court, cook and serve food, take money and make change all day long. As time went by the ships moved across the bay, a huge devastating pier fire engulfed both Piers 30 & 32 flanking the tiny funky foodery, and a complete Embarcadero face lift happened. Red's still survives.

Today Red's sits under the Bay Bridge, dominating the waterfront landscape at the head of Bryant Street as an iconic monument to the heritage of San Francisco, and goes on feeding its funky food to the fanatic funky food addicts.

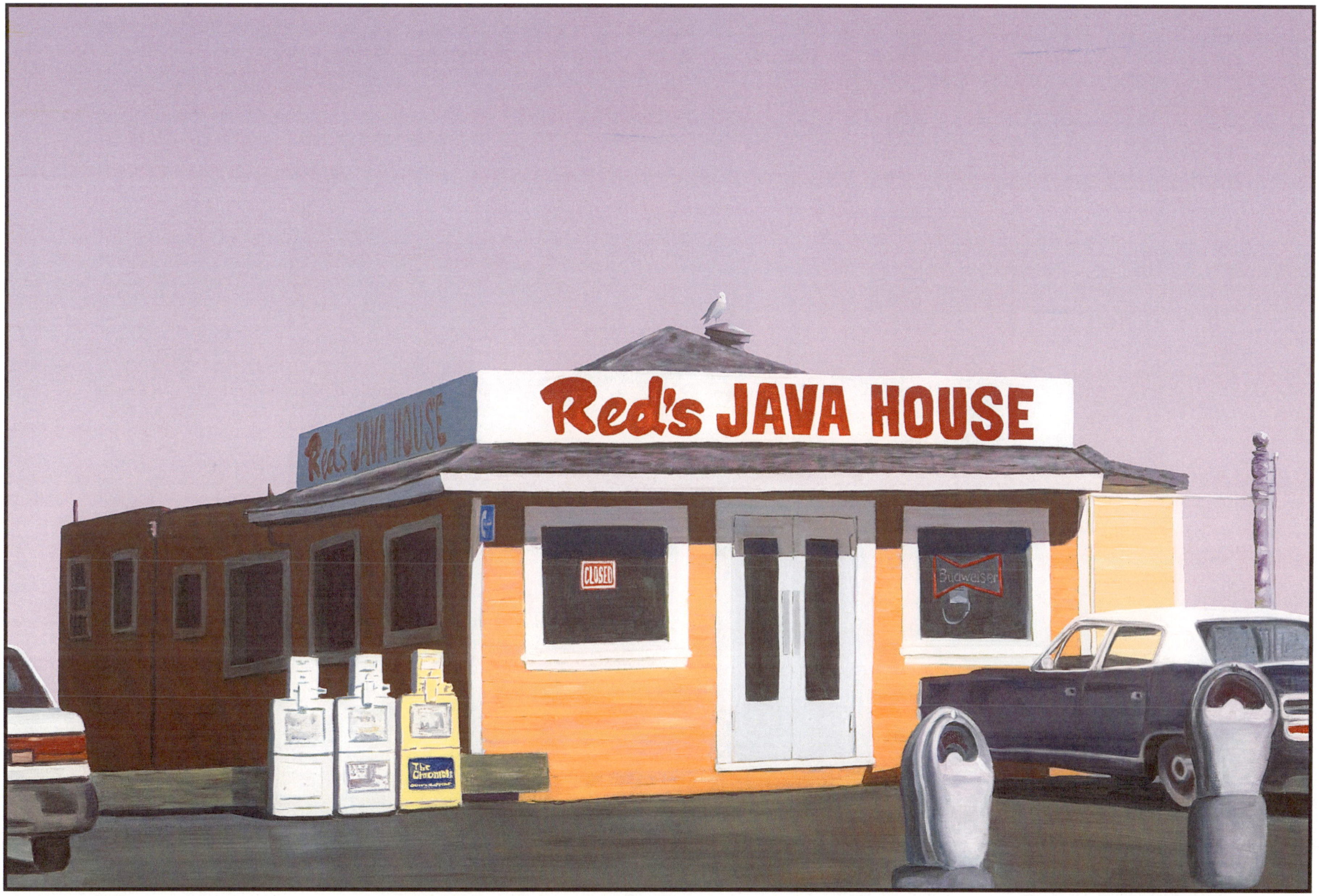

RED'S JAVA HOUSE **Oil on Canvas 4'x 5'**

WALT'S DINER

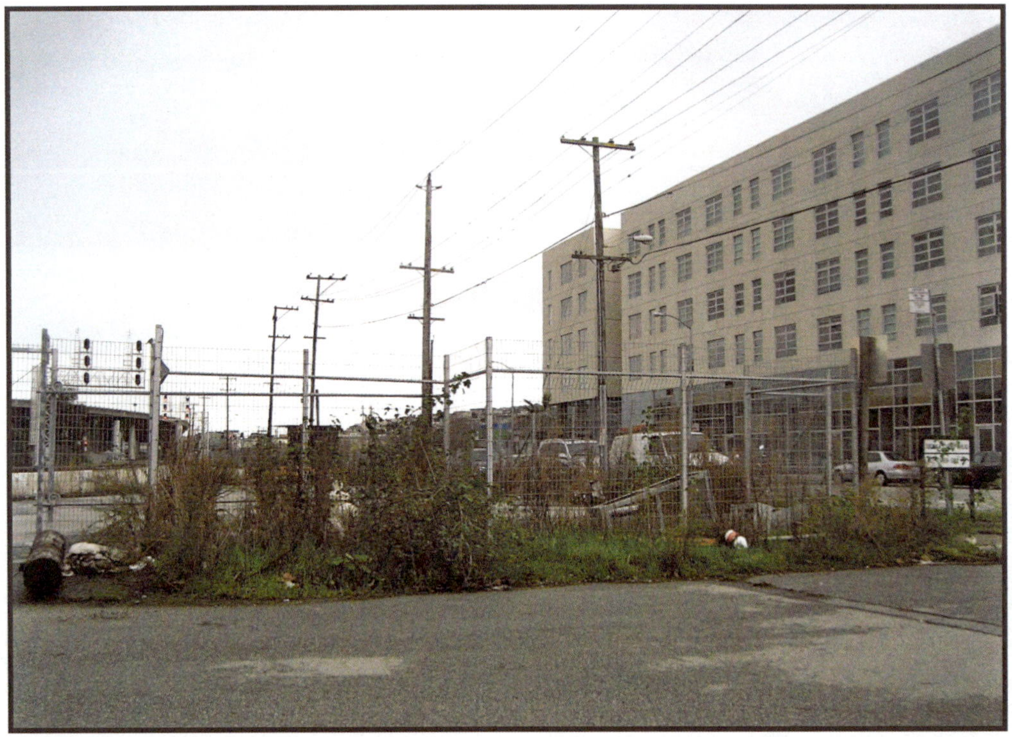

Where's Walt's?

Take a ride (or walk) down 7th Street here in San Francisco to King Street, stand on the corner and look around. All you'll see today is a place where San Francisco Muni and Caltrain stash their used street signs and park their trucks and utility vehicles.

What was once a hot little corner filled by a picturesque "Belly Bomb Shelter" called Walt's Diner is now a scrap dump. That little gourmet arsenal was stocked with hearty chili, hot Java, cold sandwiches, overcooked burgers, greasy fries, and a warm hello on a cold San Franciscan day.

Patronized by hard working waterfront longshoremen and warehousemen, Walt's was a welcome oasis in the middle of a steel and concrete desert. Perched on the former edge of the city just south of Townsend Street, it fed the folks that sat inside or at little tables along the tracks as well as the quickies who grabbed grub at the takeout counter.

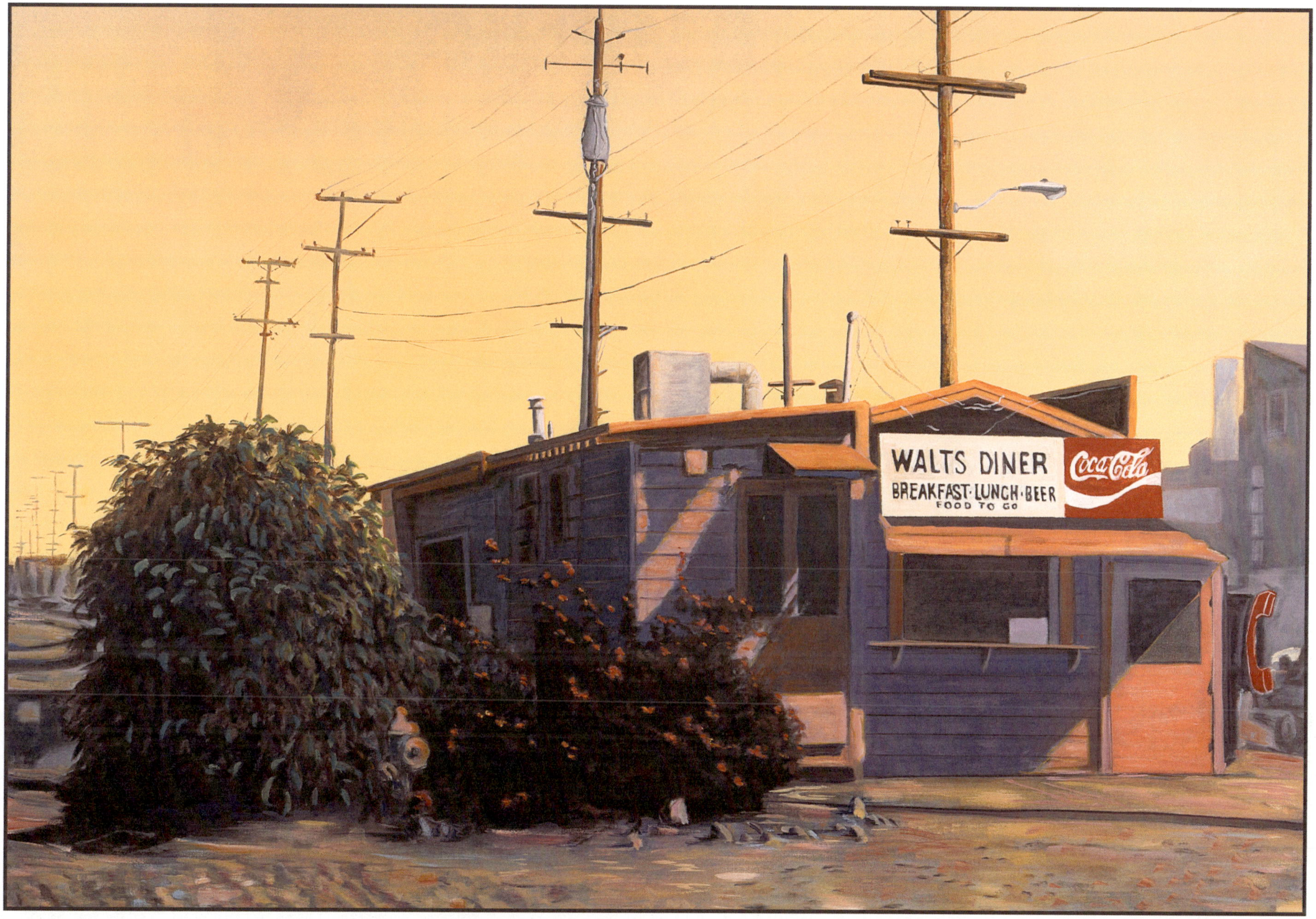

WALT'S DINER Oil on Canvas 4'x 5'

CARMEN'S

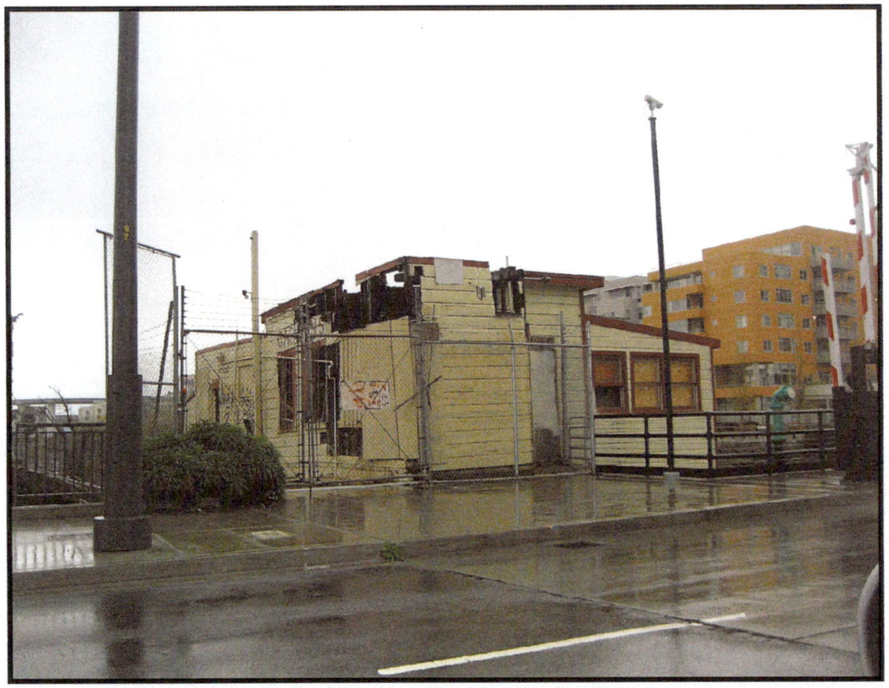

Carmen's Bites the Dust

In the 60's and 70's it was called Blanche's, a famous spot for artists and bohemians. Then Carmen took it over and maintained its artistic integrity until the Mission Bay Project got the land and began "developing" it.

After years of reigning as an artists' hangout, today Carmen's is a vacant memory standing shallow at the edge of the slough next to the Fourth Street Bridge. It sat empty, idle and burnt out for a long time waiting for the future to deterine its destiny. And the wrecking ball of the future did.

Now it is gone.

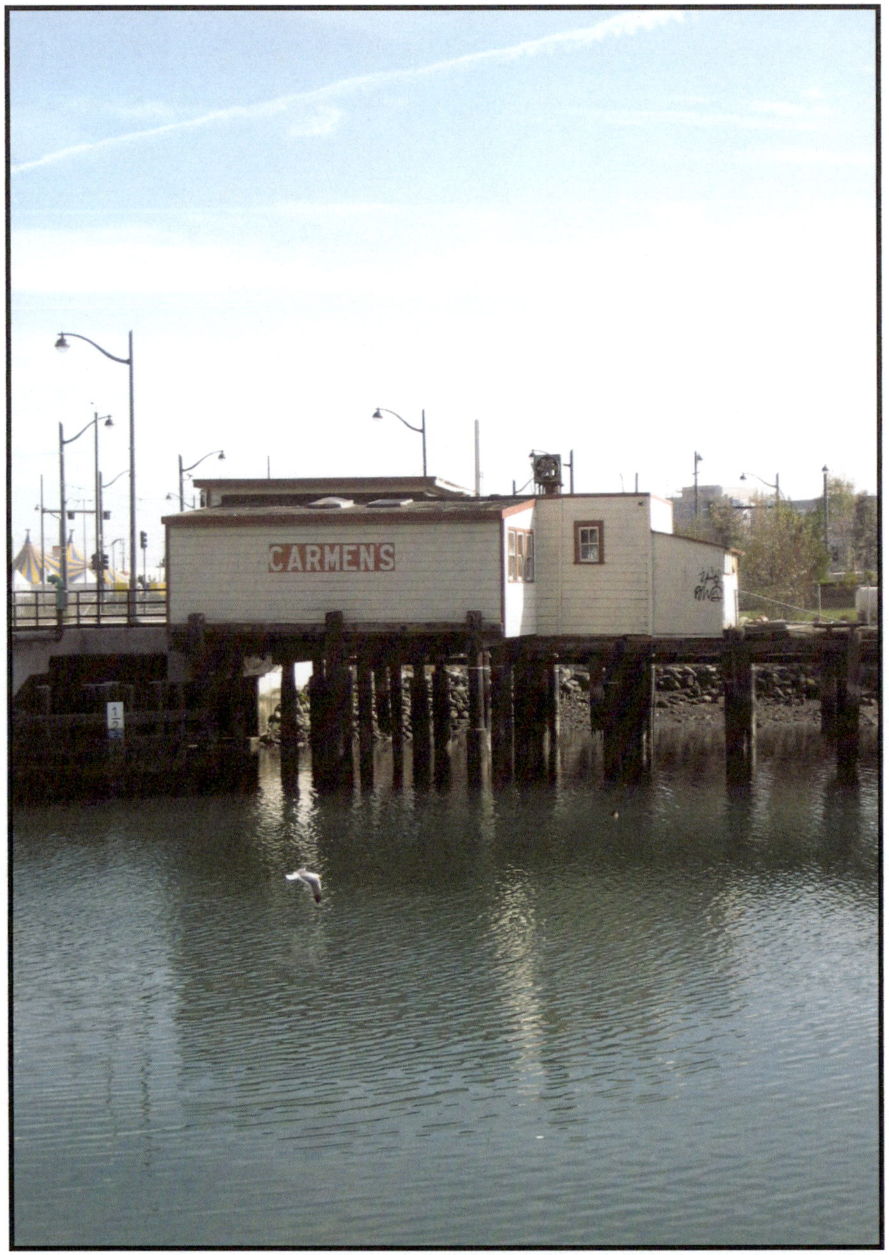

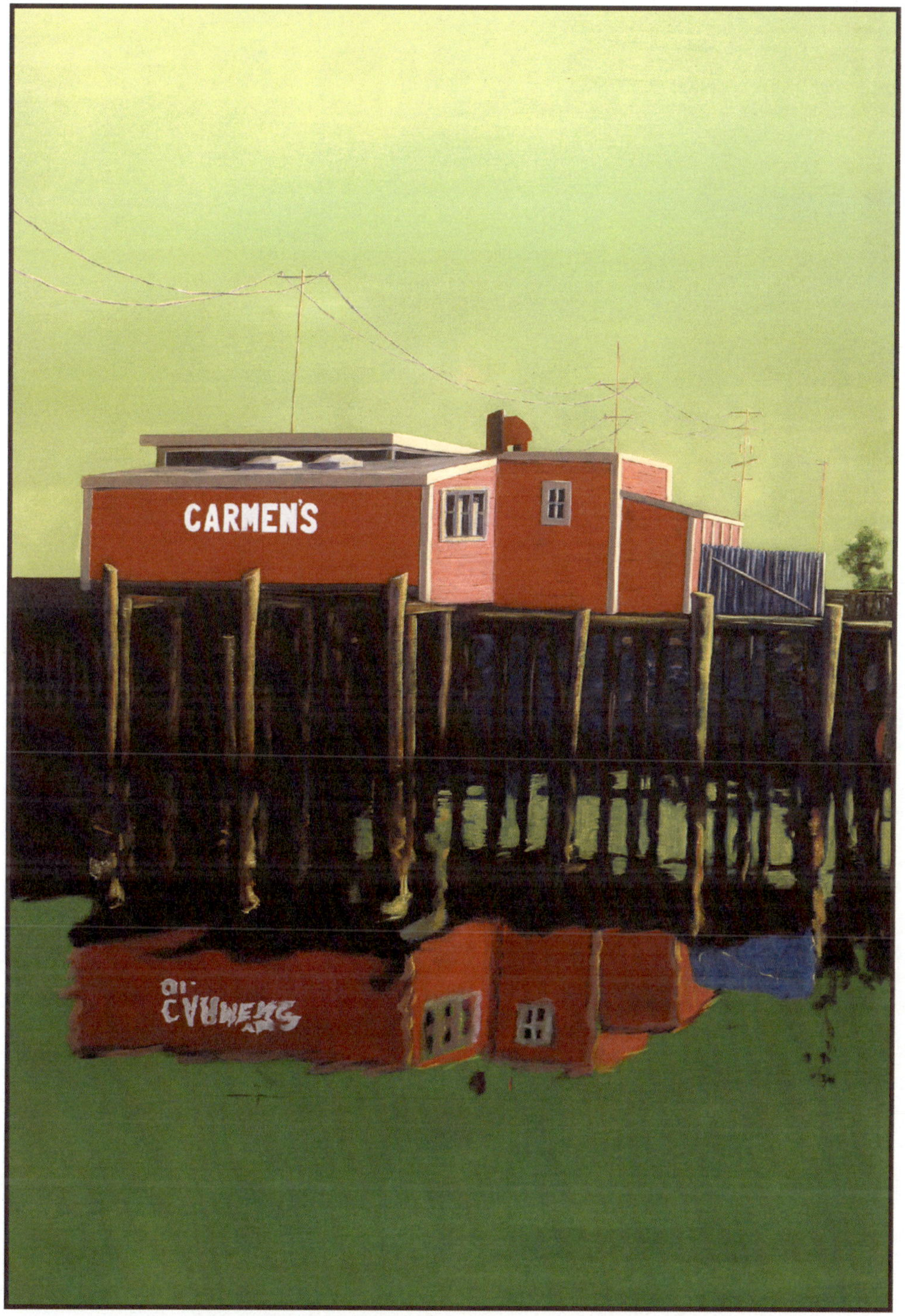

CARMEN'S Oil on Canvas 4'x 5'

TRIANGLE SANDWICH SHOP

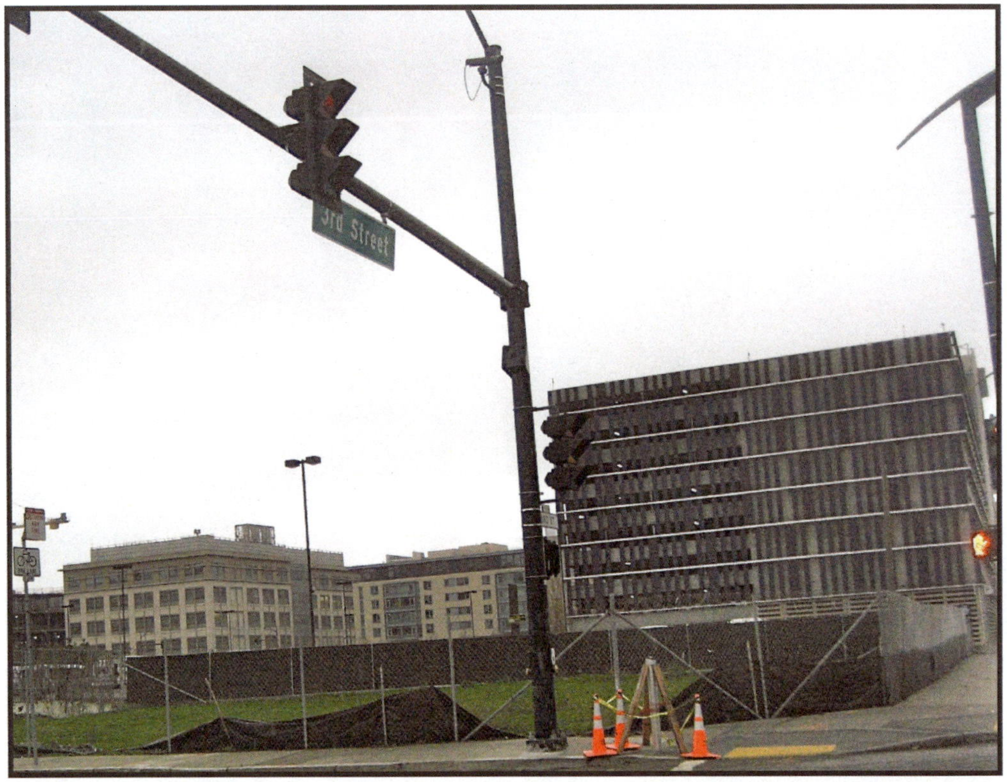

The Triangle Loses Its Edge

Swallowed up by the Mission Bay Project, The Triangle Sandwich Shop took its last bite in 2006.

Low on quality, fast on service, high on friendship, this joint brought in the fast moving trucker and travel crowd. Salty ship and steel workers would grind down the grilled grub and suck up the salty suds dished out in this triangular shaped mecca planted at the corner of 16th and 3rd Streets.

Now gone, and rolled over by the biotech brains, costly condos, sport stadiums, medical machines and parking lots, its memory still casts a melancholy shadow on the lost souls who chowed down there.

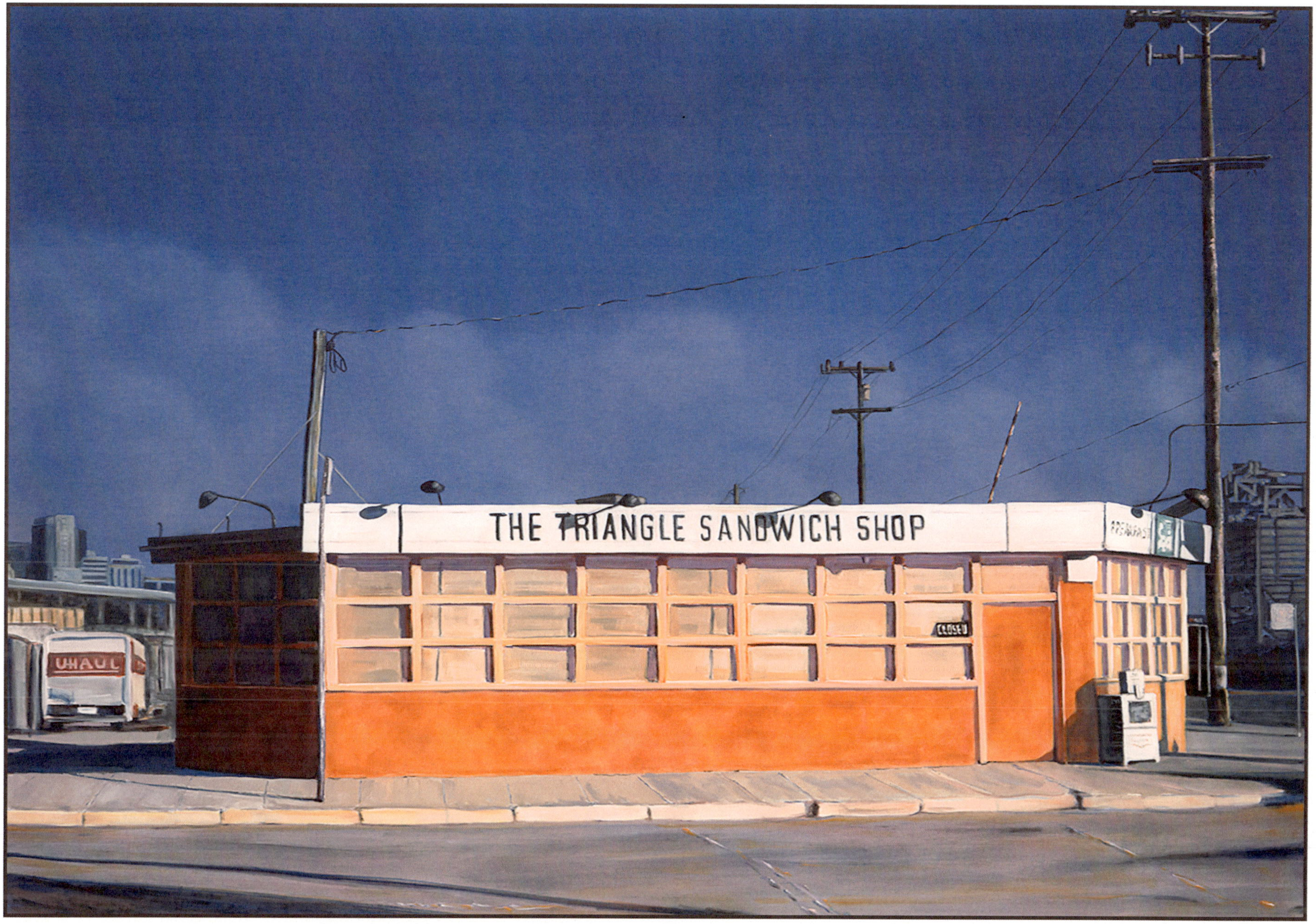

THE TRIANGLE SANDWICH SHOP Oil on Canvas 4′x 5′

JAVA HOUSE

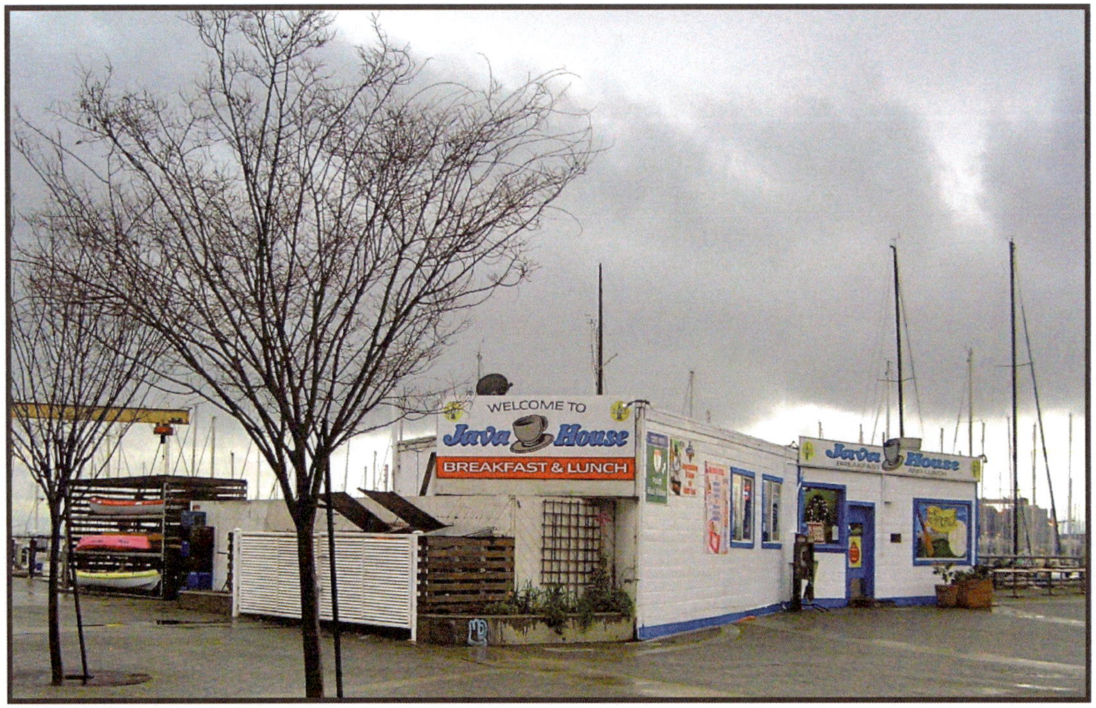

Welcome to Java House

This little monument to gastronomy invites its patrons to the hearty hunky grub it's been dishing out for over 60 years. For a long time this long wooden hut was tucked away at the mouth of the Mission Bay Slough along the tracks of the Belt Line Railroad feeding the same rough crew of blue collar boys all the other Java Joints served.

But as the Embarcadero rose from the depths of industrial ambiance, Java House rode the wave. Now its alabaster prominence sticks out at the curve in the road near swanky bistros, chuck wagons, watering holes and huge crowds that spill out of the baseball games from the "Phone Booth," aka AT&T Ball Park.

Java House almost lost its lease when in 2007 the Port Commission tried to jack up the rent about 5 times and get a percentage of the action. But the people rose up. Matier and Ross from the ***San Fransico Chronicle*** blew the whistle and Java House survived.

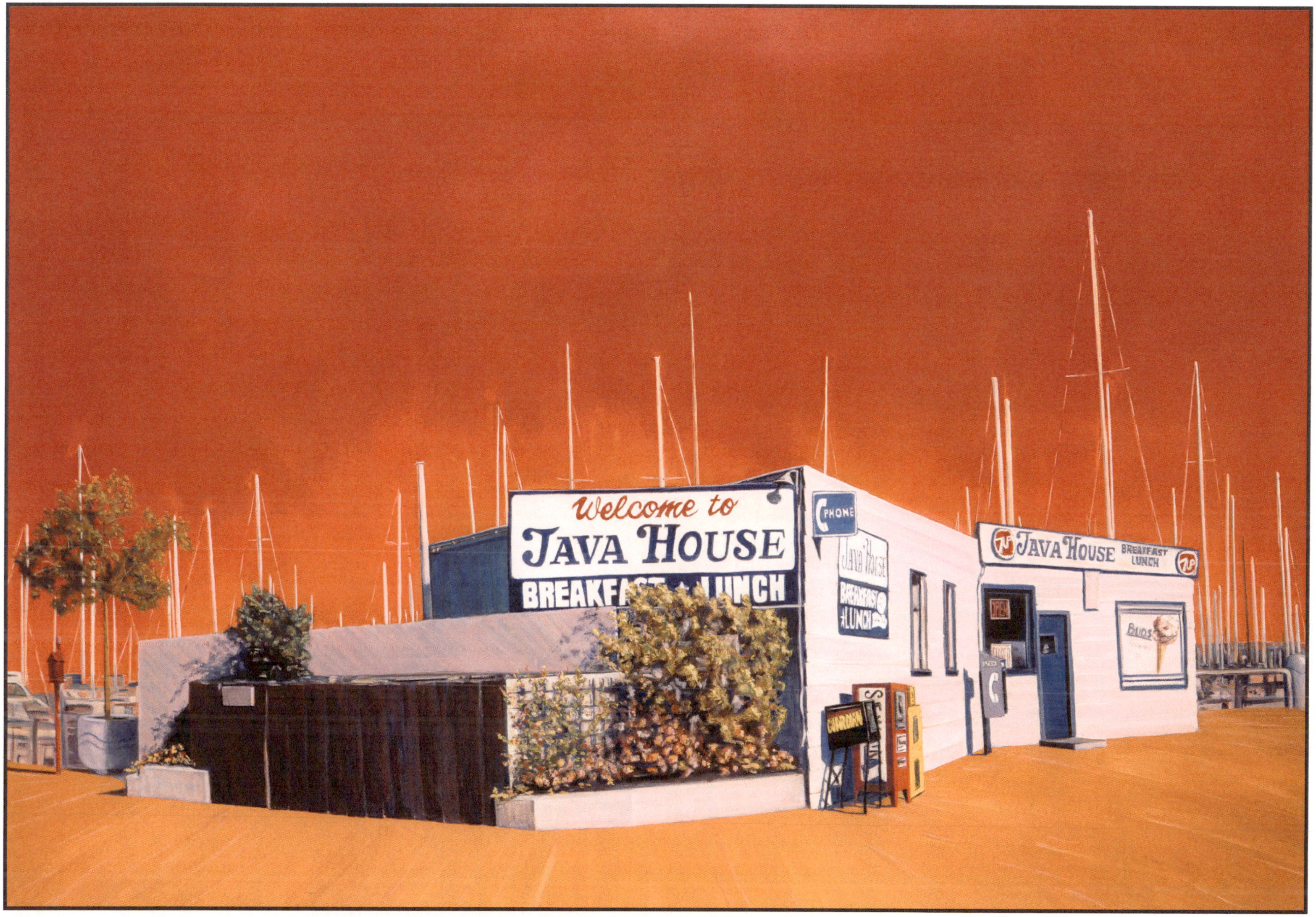

WELCOME TO JAVA HOUSE **Oil on Canvas 4′x 5′**

PIER 23

Jazzy Java Joint

Hey check it out! There's a live band at Pier 23 . . . pounding out a beat down on the waterfront.

An old time longshoreman's hangout and dine in, this joint also passed the test of time, dishing out grub that sticks against the girth of any health food fanatic for a long time.

Now under the careful culinary eyes of Flicka McGurrin and her son, Mac McGurrin, it's a rocking good club, cooking with music and fine food filling the guts of natives and visitors as they chow down on the dock of the Bay.

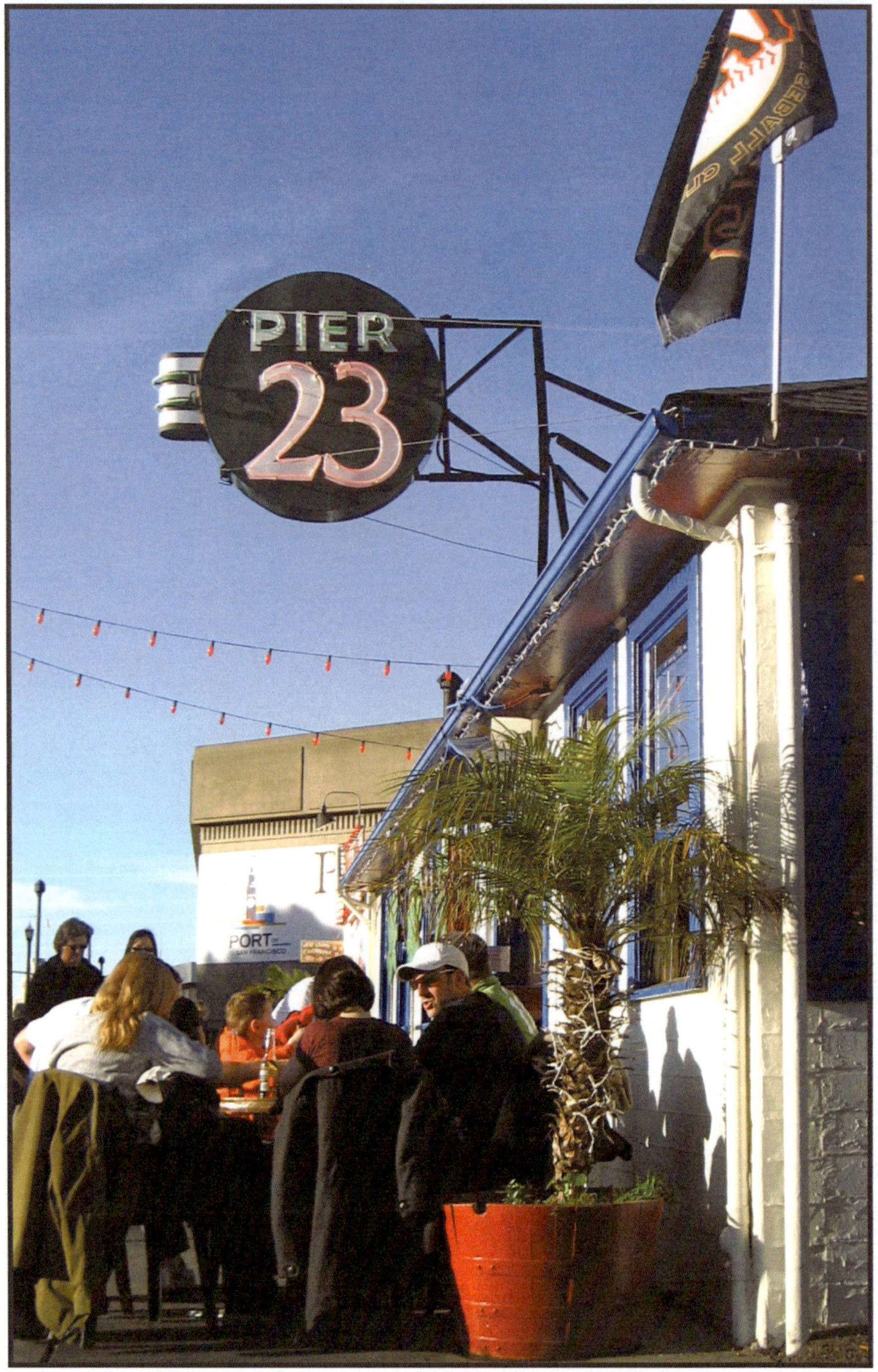

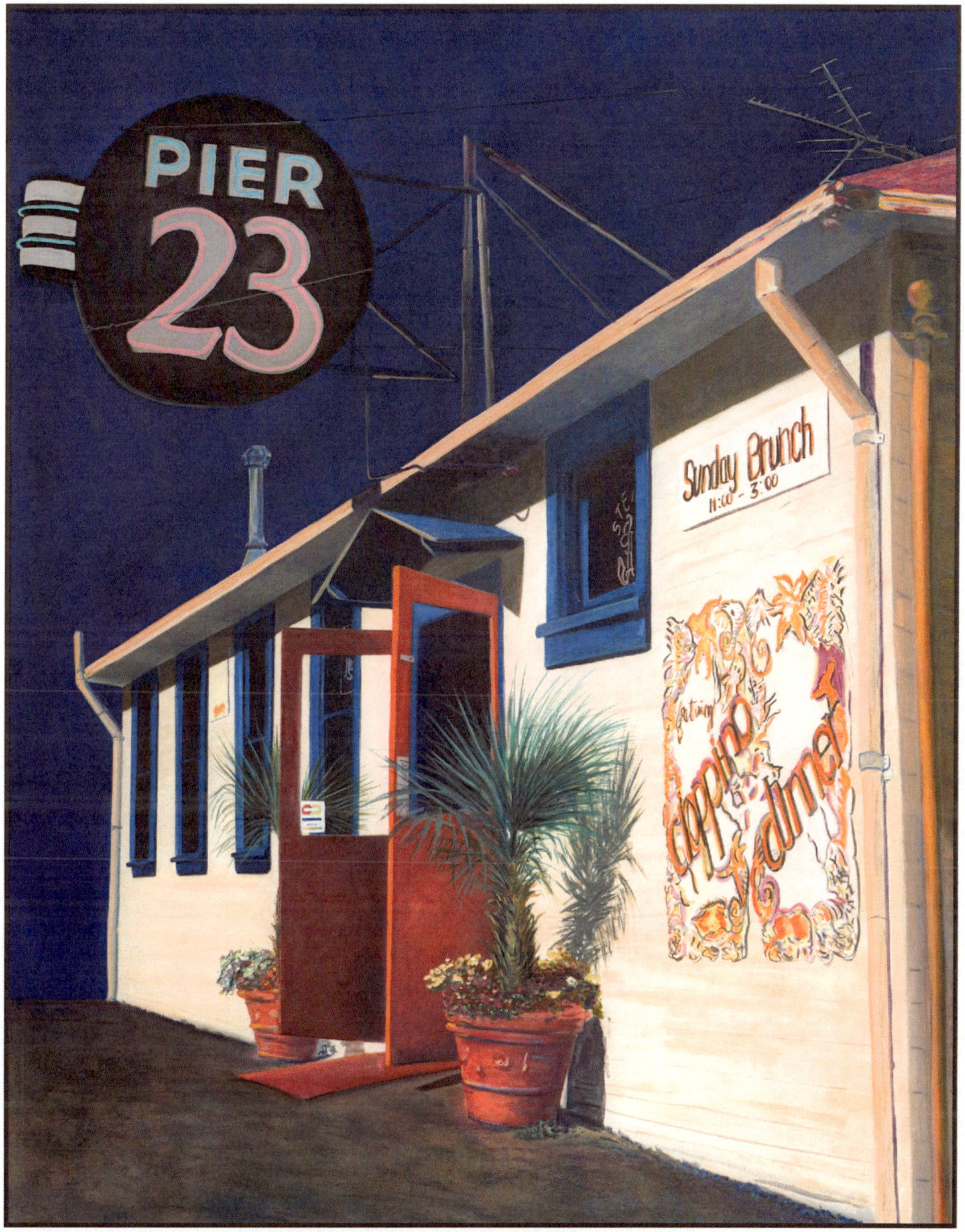

PIER 23 **Oil on Canvas 4′x 5′**

WOLFE'S LUNCH

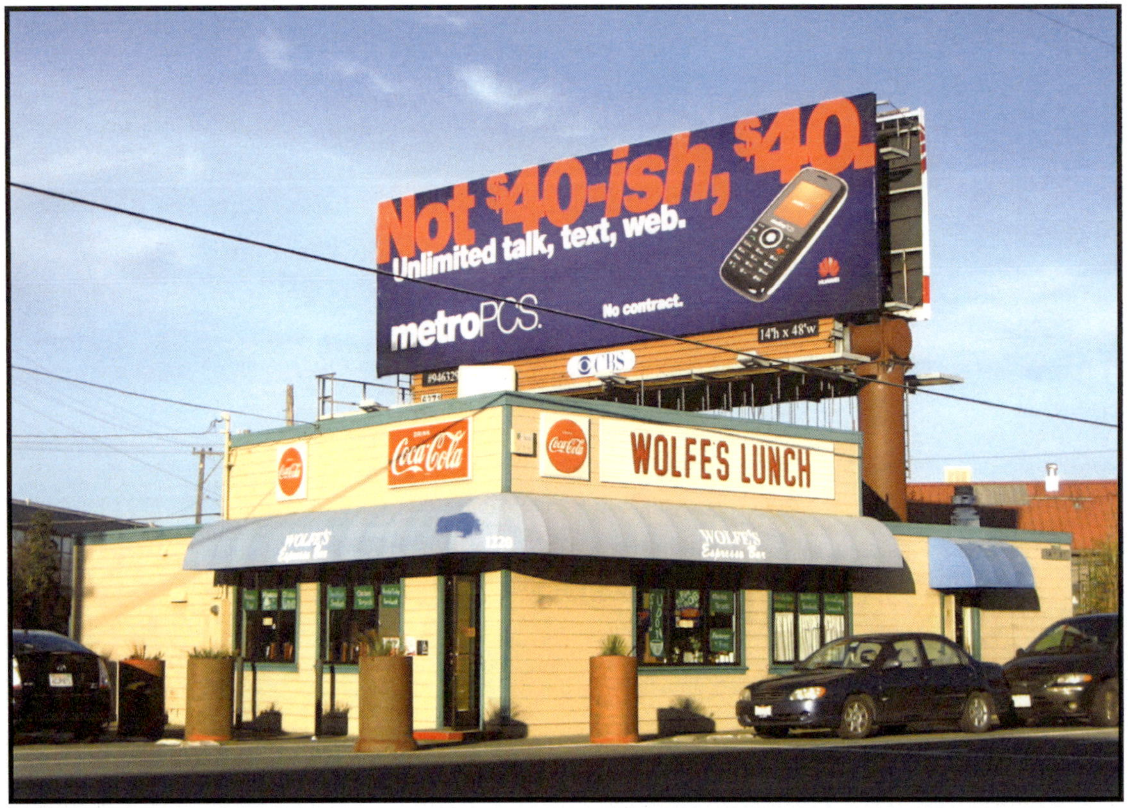

Wolfe's Gets A Nose Job

Long before the turn of the 21st century, Wolfe's was a den for blue-collar truckers to pull up to and dig into some hearty grub and hot coffee. Nestled on the triangle of 16th Street and Arkansas at the foot of Potrero Hill, this little gourmet trapezoid catered to the folks that broke their backs along the bustling industrial routes of the south of Market section.

Then came the Dot Commers and the fashion icons and overnight the red brick warehouses enclosed a totally different product and with it came the finer palates of the fashion fanatics. From blue collars to pink collars, chic cafés and restaurants popped up and Wolfe's had a face lift. It converted its bull-nosed facade into a right angle and from its trapezoid shape it scrapped its front door phone booths and expanded into the triangular look it has now, meeting the new breed of artsy fashionistas with its down home simple Asiatic fare.

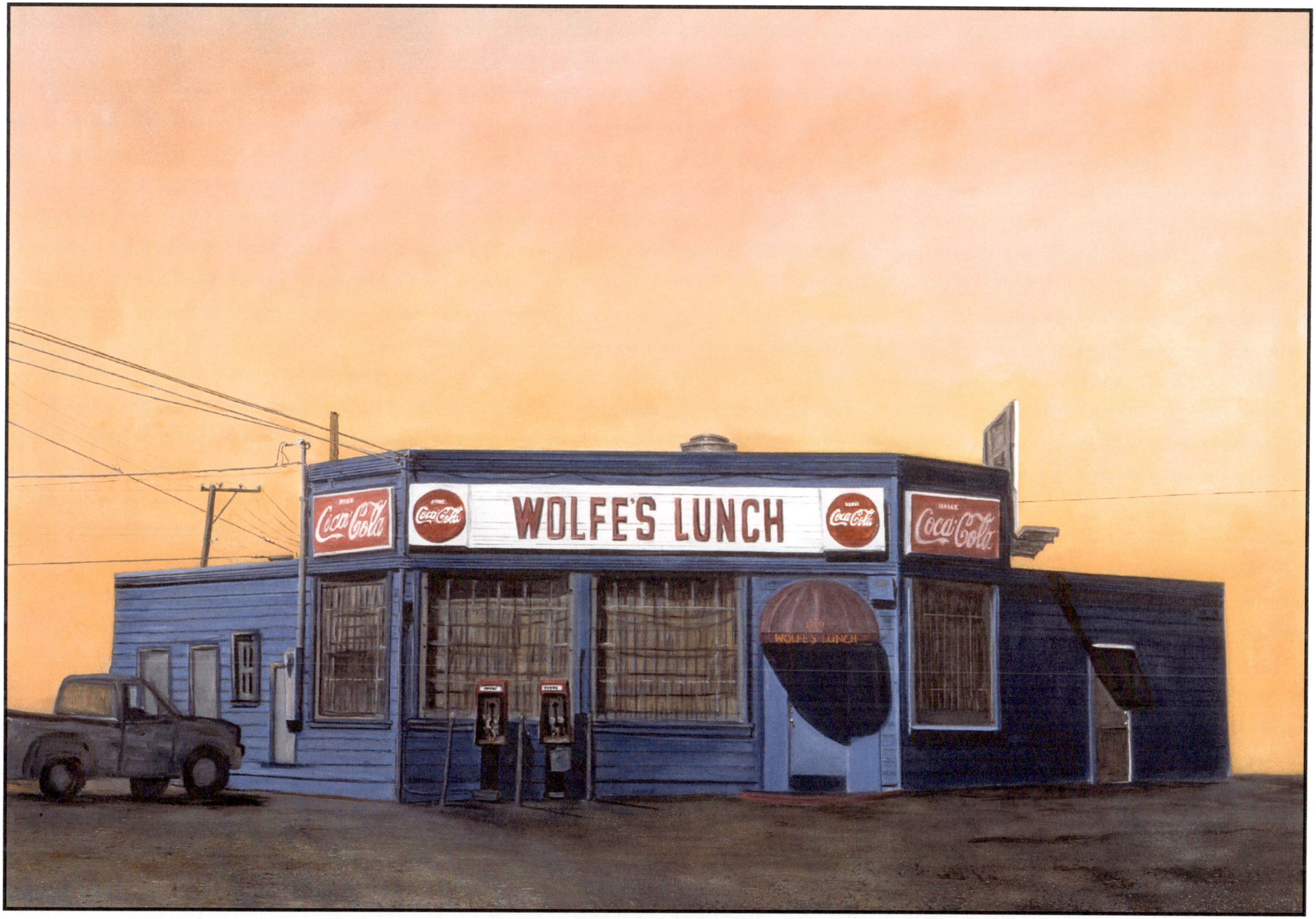

WOLFE'S LUNCH **Oil on Canvas 4'x 5'**

BONANZA

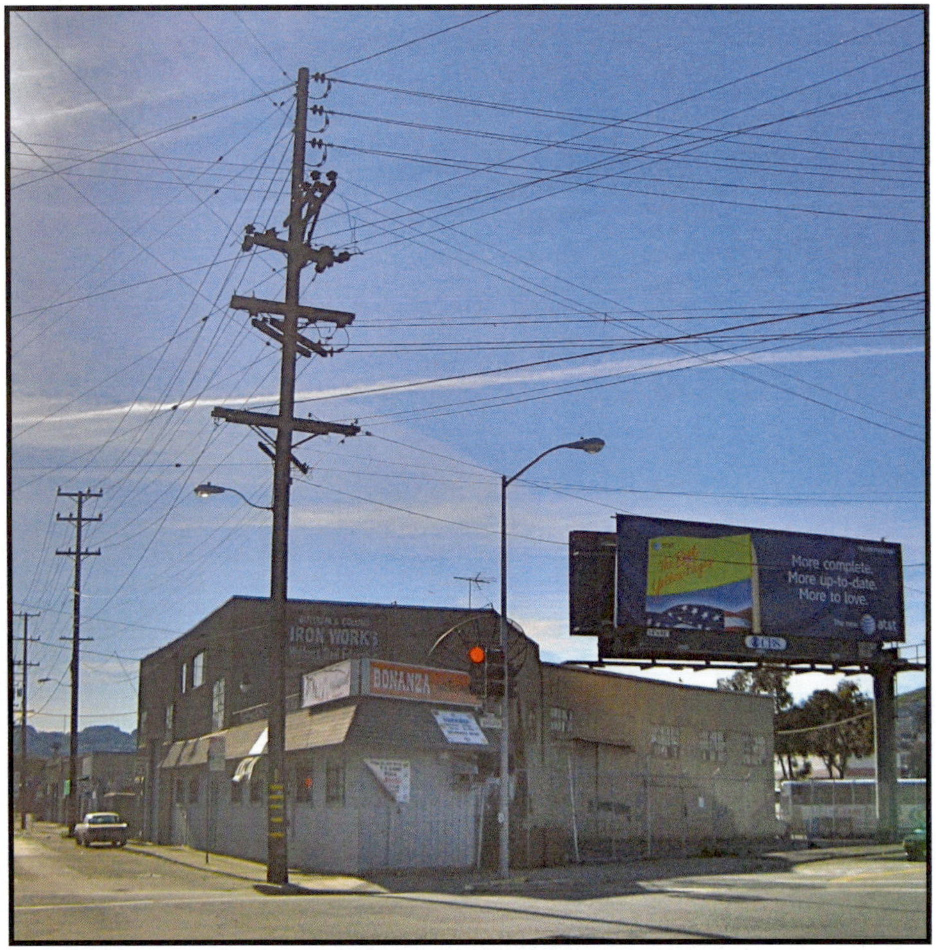

Dig Deep

Tucked way down on the south side of town, a block below old Army (Caesar Chavez) Street at the junction of Toland, Evans and Napoleon Streets, stands the Bonanza. Once a haven for hungry and thirsty farmers' marketeers and bakers from the Parisian bakery next door, this little mother lode of a bar and restaurant quenched the thirst and appetites of those hardy patrons.

Now closed and still sitting tight under strings of high power wires and lanes of bending telephone poles, the Bonanza was a rich strike for its steady luncheon customers and traveling whiskey miners looking for a friendly place to park their axes.

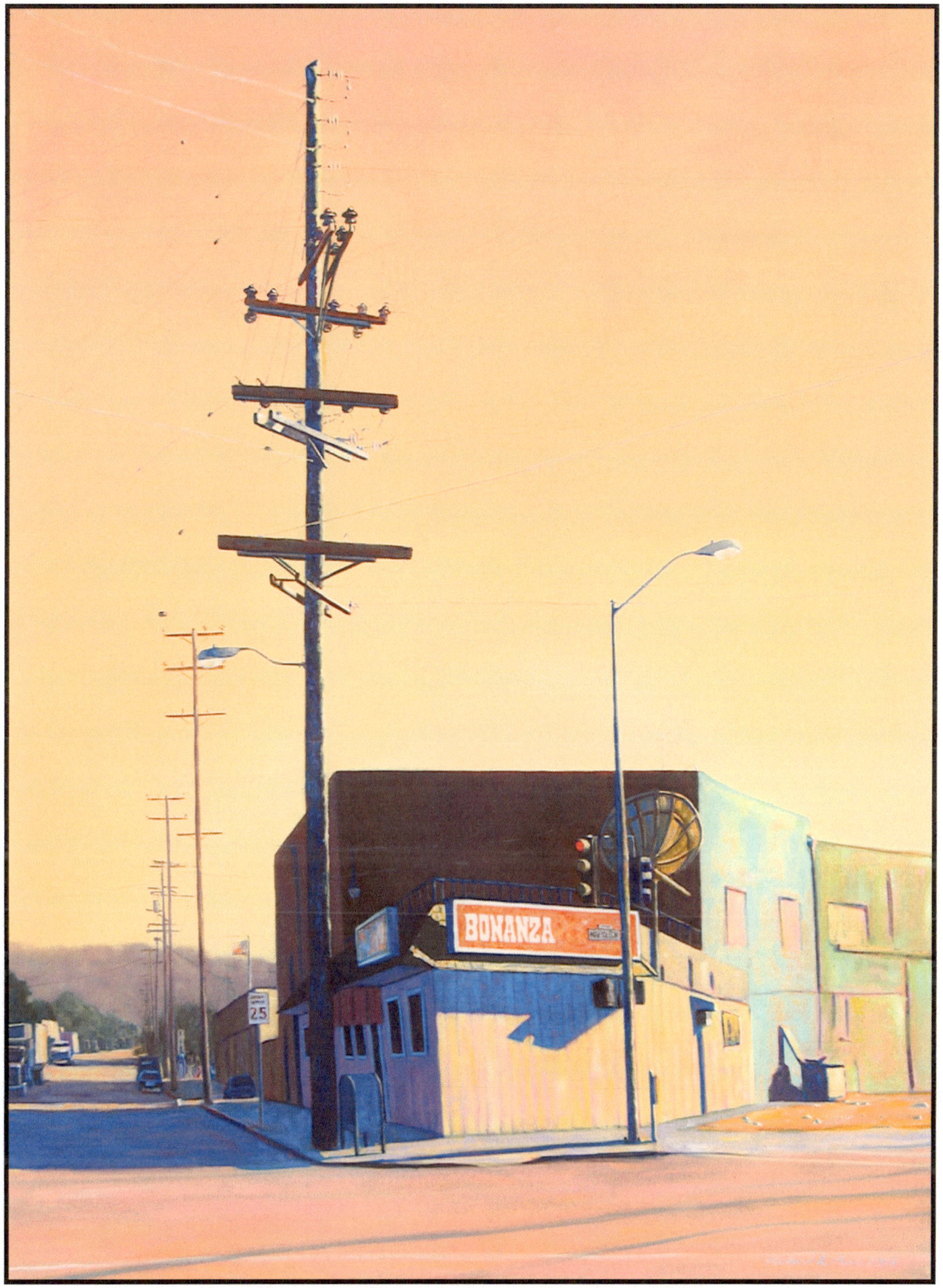

BONANZA Oil on Canvas 4'x 5'

THE WHIZ

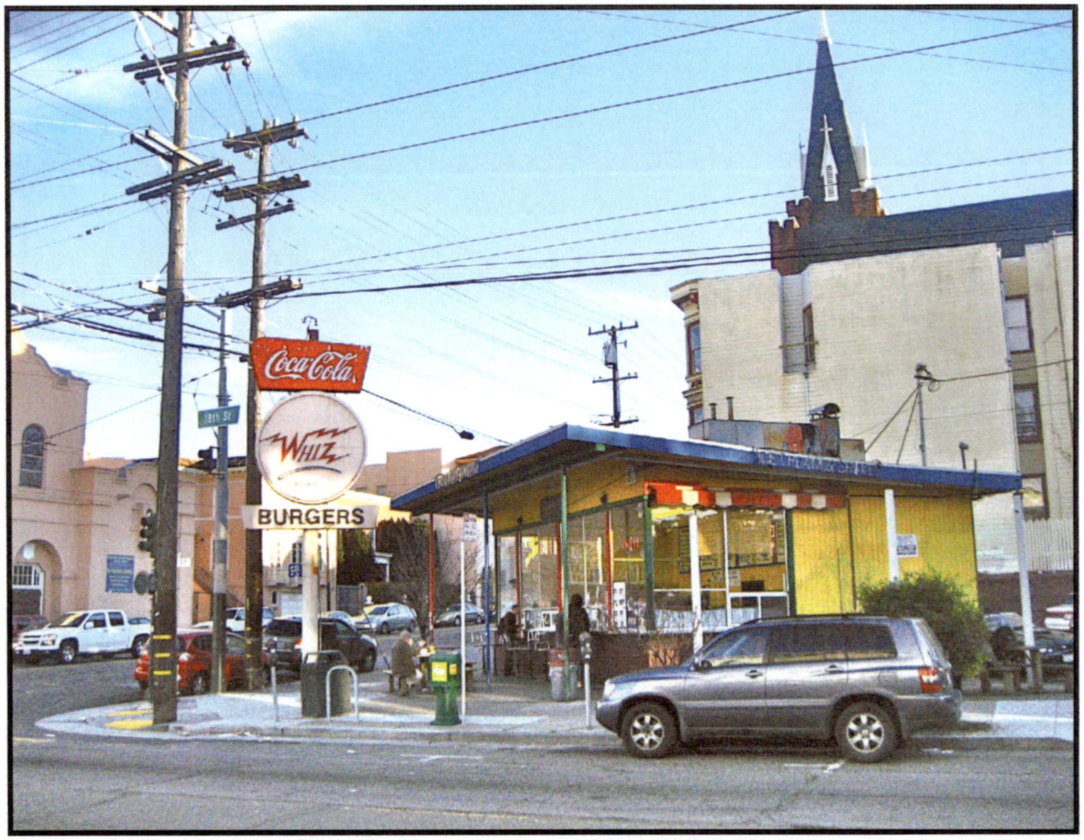

The Wizardly Wonder of South Van Ness

Most native San Franciscans and transplanted long-term residents know what The Whiz is.

Once upon a time an old mansion sat on this spot until the middle of last century when John and Fred Hider took it out of probate and erected this fashionable 19-cent burger palace. Sitting in the Mission district on the corner of South Van Ness and 18th Street, this classic drive-in fills the famished fast-food aficionados with a good helping of greasy fries and flamed out, flipped up burgers.

All cities have them and San Francisco does too.

This section of town is definitely a drive-in mecca for meat mongers who meander the streets seeking some fast warm food or quick hot pleasure and whatever you want. All you need to do is drive up to The Whiz and get it.

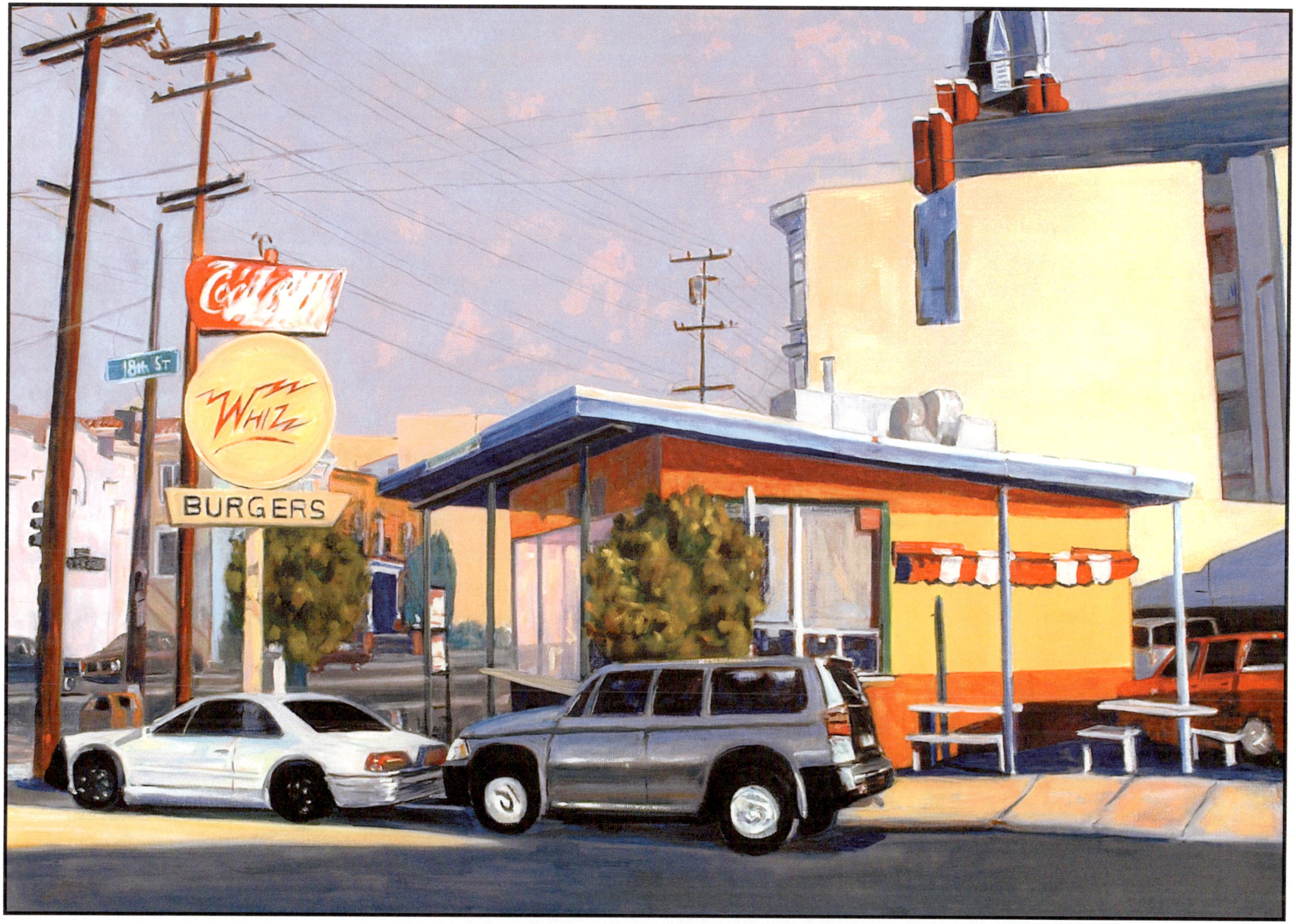

THE WHIZ Oil on Canvas 4′x 5′

3rd STREET STATION

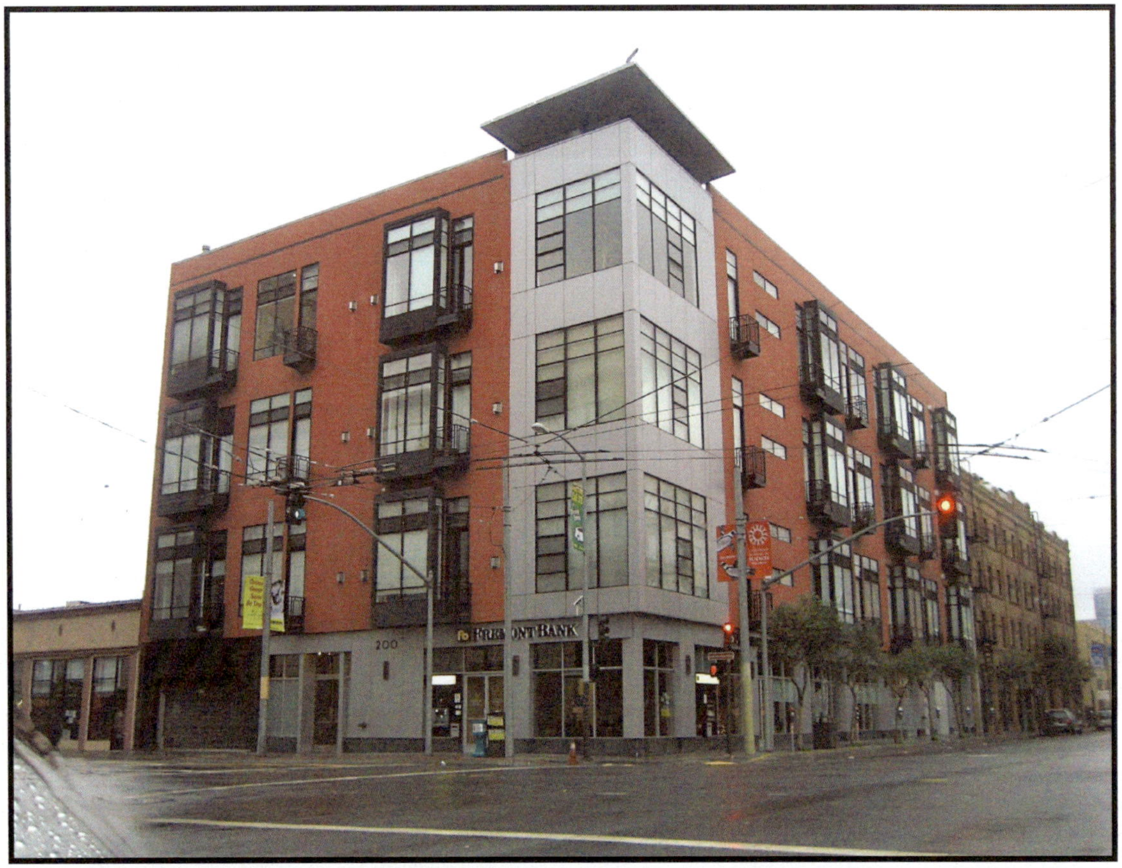

3rd Street Station Rolls Outta Town

Once the 3rd Street Station was the commuter's first or last watering hole to and from the office in downtown San Francisco. Now it's magically transformed into a bank with a three story condo crown. The 3rd Street Station was right across the street from the majestically old classic Southern Pacific train station that loomed large on 3rd Street between Brannan and Townsend.

Commuters would flow into the 3rd Street Station Bar and pour the booze down their throats to bone up for the daily office grind or the train ride home.

But, alas, the wrecking ball sang out its last call and 3rd Street Station raised its glass up to modern 21st-century architecture.

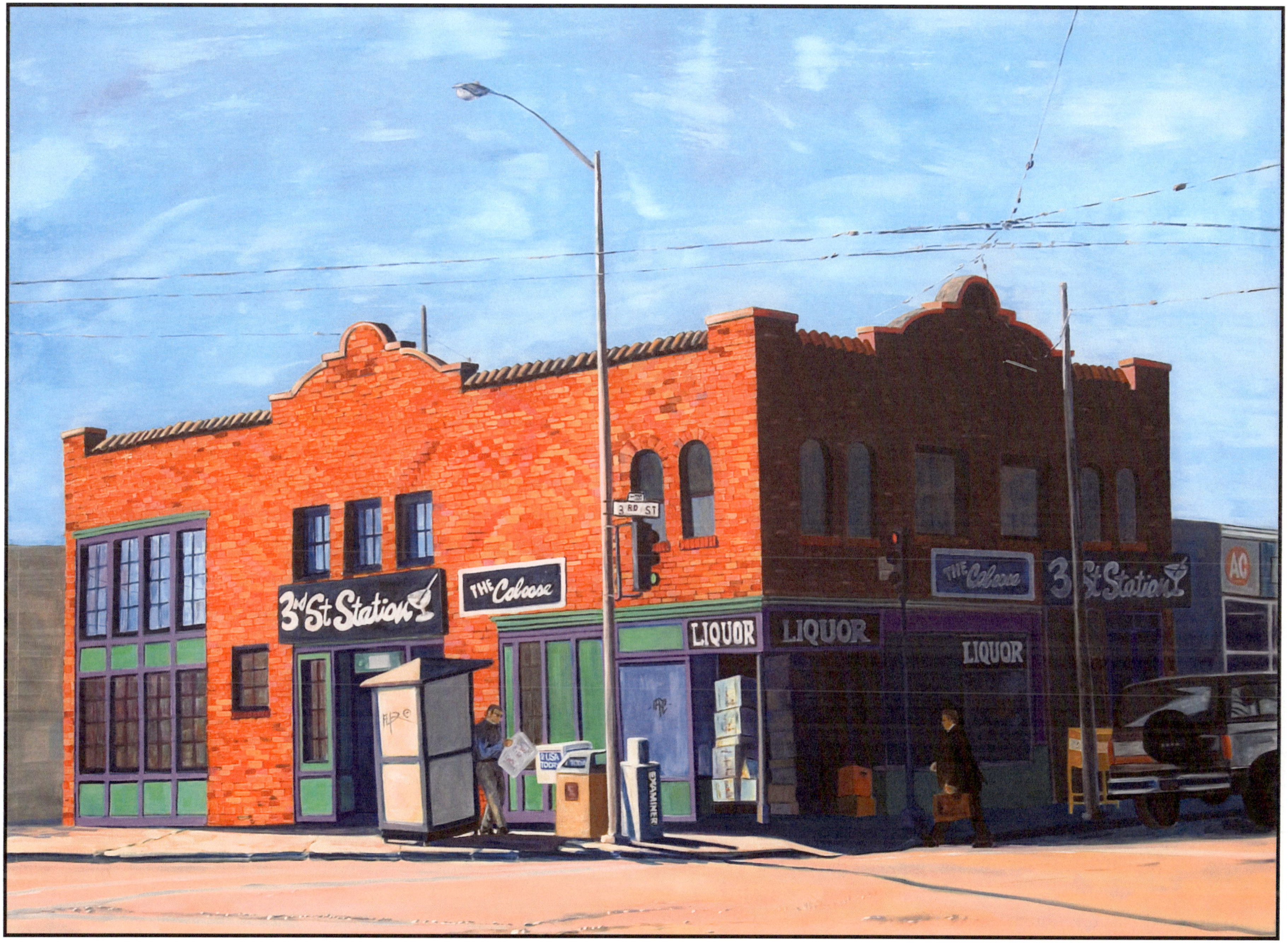

3rd STREET STATION Oil on Canvas 5′x 6′

BRAIN WASH

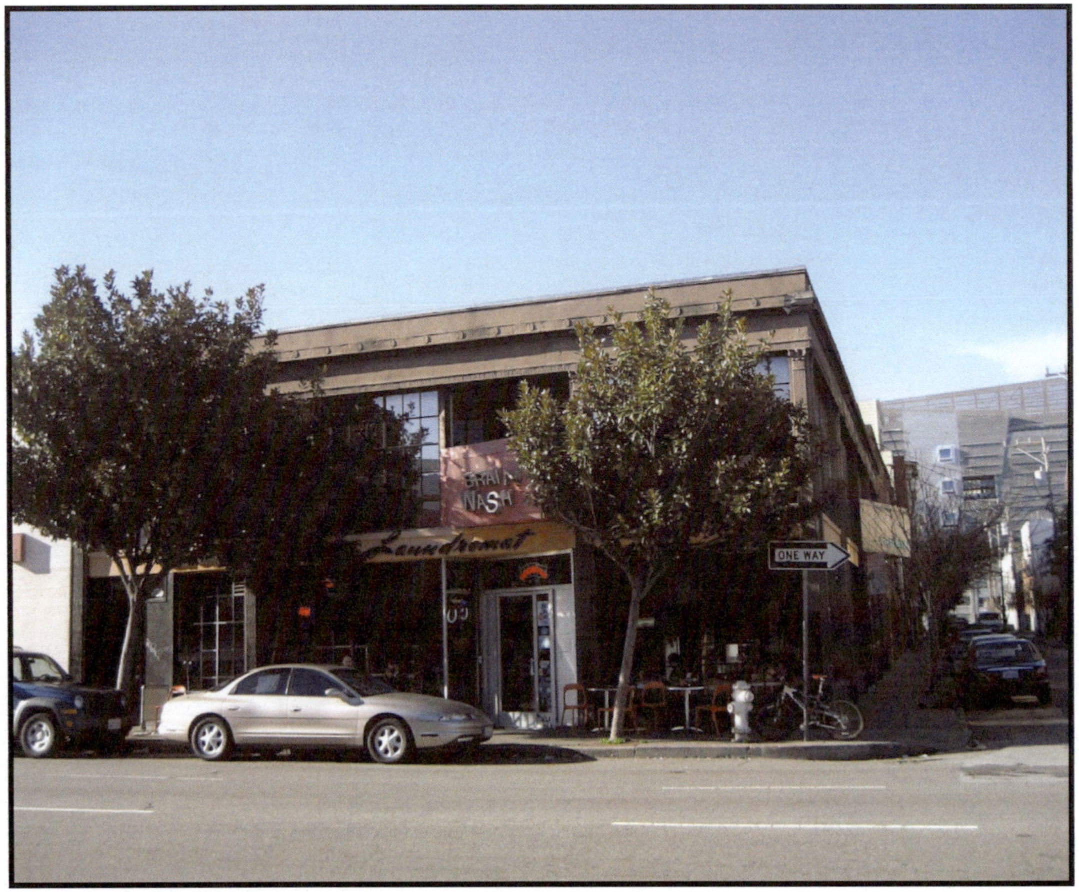

Birthplace of the "Washeraunts"

Folsom and 7th Street, a small hub of hipsterism, held on to three distinct girth growing gardens. Brain Wash was the cleanest of these, a place where the cool cleaning crowd came to wash up their clothes with coin operated machines and wash down their meals with coin bought grub and suds.

The brainchild of Susan Schindler, Brain Wash had become a benchmark for other washaurants and started the clean food trend. In addition to the wash and food, Brain Wash hosted music and art shows interspersed with live poetry and other performance activities all done by local talent. It was a great place to hang out, be entertained and clean up.

Alas today, Brain Wash is gone and washed out.

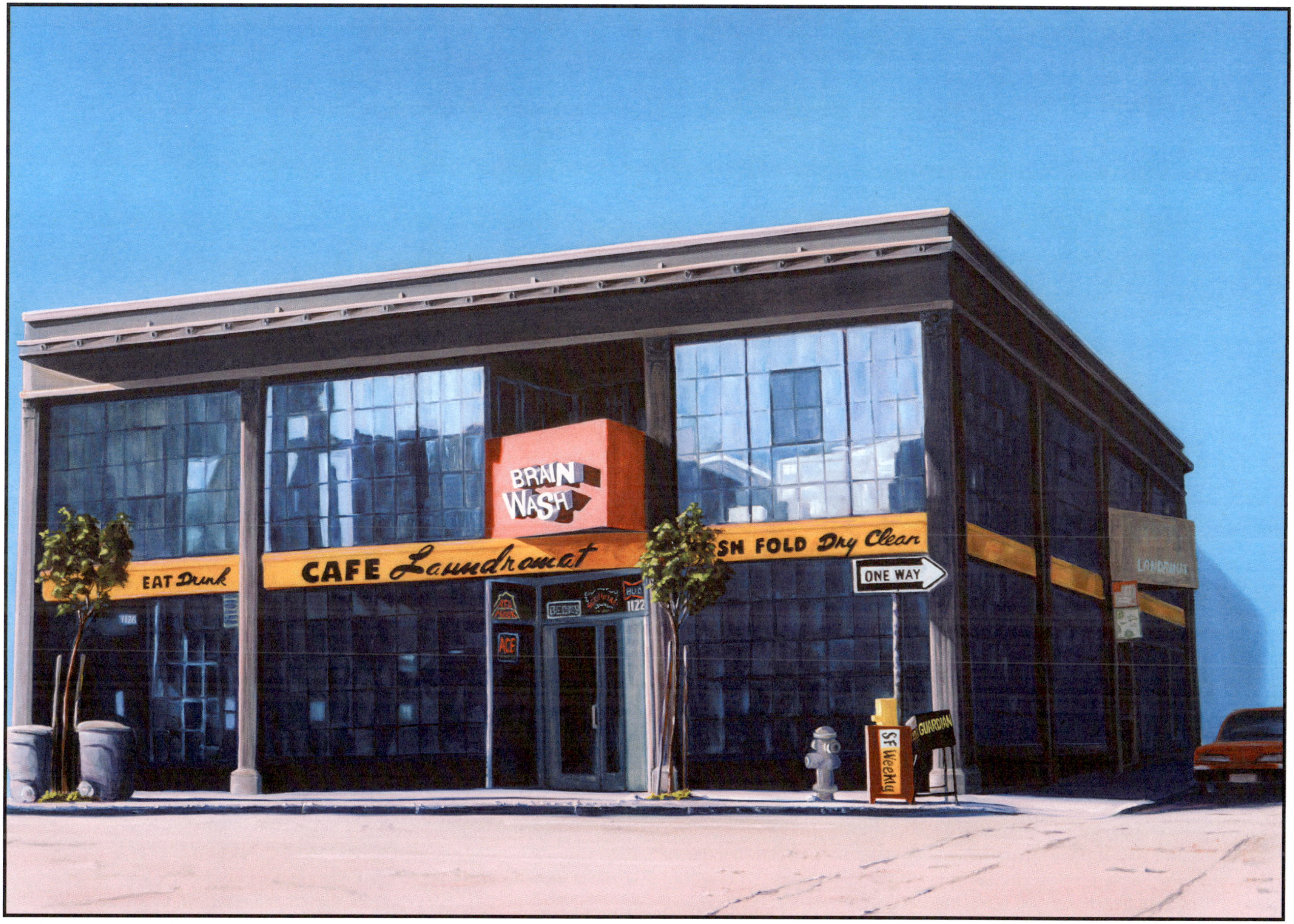

BRAIN WASH Oil on Canvas 4′x 5′

THE OLD MINT

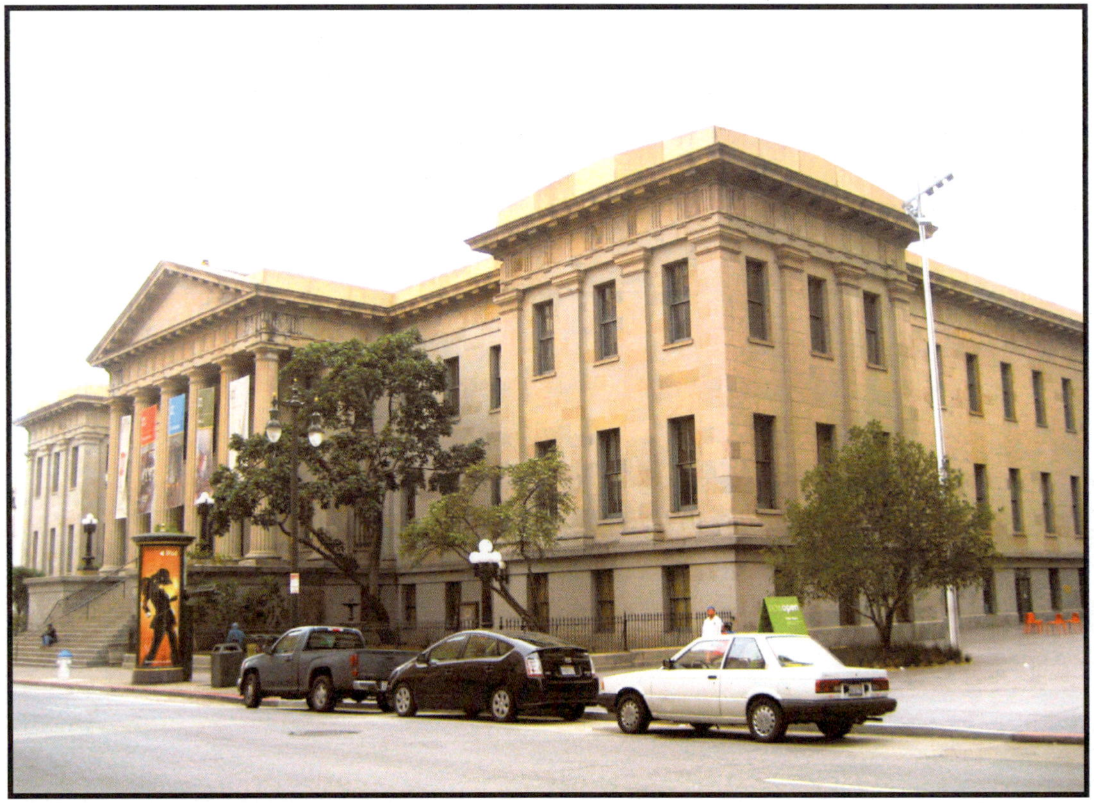

Monumental Money Maker

At 5th and Mission Streets, the monetary master of numismatology still stamps out its presence. The Old Mint is a monument to San Francisco's heritage and is an excellent example of Neo-French Classic architecture.

This old money mansion lay vacant and partially abandoned after the shake of 1989 and became a hideout for bums and junkies. Then, in 2005, things began to change and it was magically turned into a museum.

The San Francisco Historical Society and the San Francisco Museum merged and set up shop here. Mr. Charles Fraccia, Chairman of the Board, recommended that the old mint be reopened with an art exhibit. The word got out and San Francisco Chronicle staff writer Carl Nolte wrote "MUSEUM LENDS QUARTERS TO ARTIST," and I was the first artist to have a one man exhibit at this new venue. It was a great opening and thousands of people came.

Now, there's a plaza in the alley flanked with fine restaurants, shops and benches among the landscaping, and its presence is circulating again.

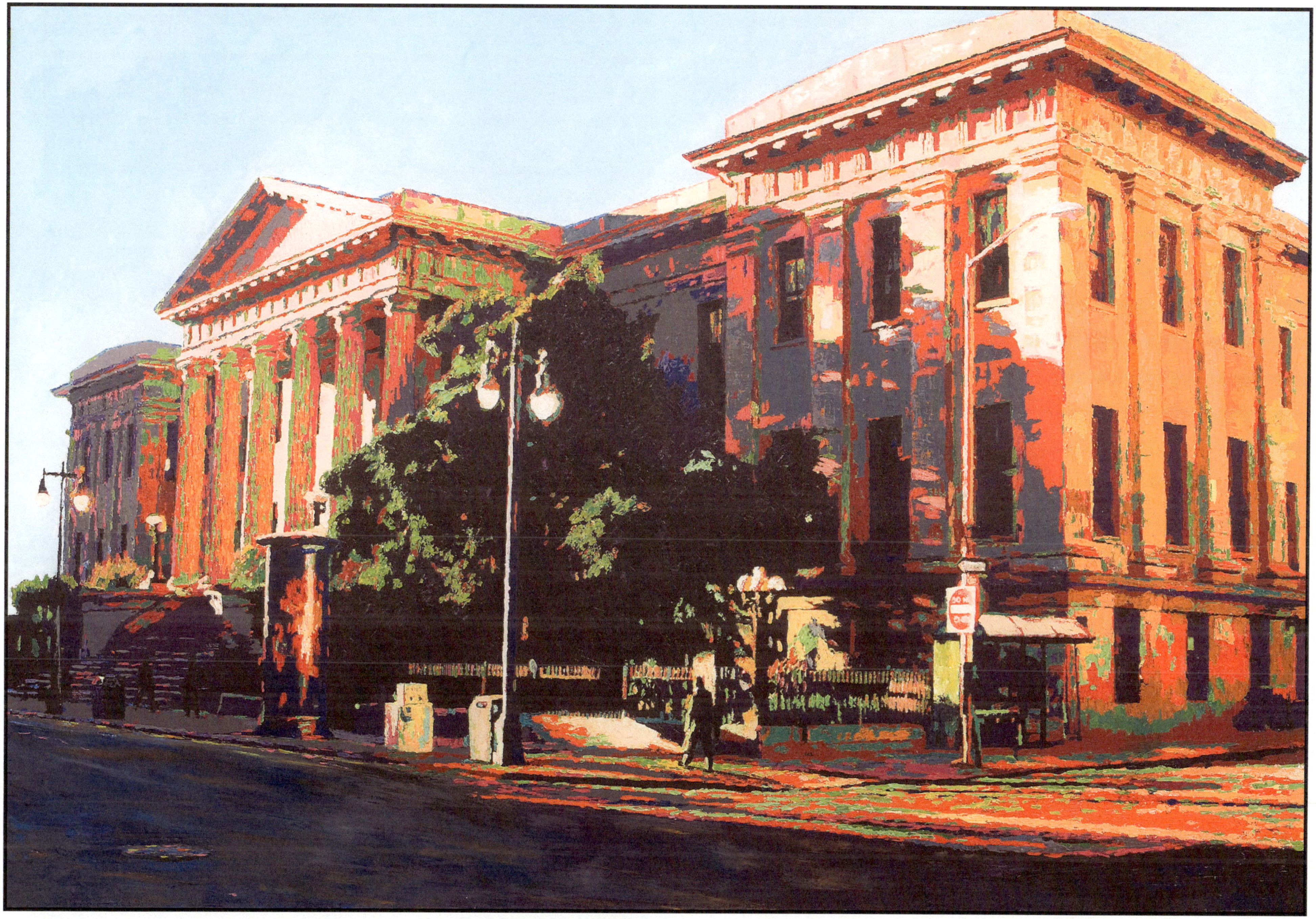

THE OLD MINT Oil on Canvas 4′x 5′

4th STREET BRIDGE

"Hey . . . Raise da Bridge"

Since 1917, the 4th Street Bridge cleared the way for millions of slow moving boats slipping in and out of the slough dividing Mission Bay from the south side of the city. Then, shortly after the turn of the century, it disappeared!!! This huge massive Basquille draw bridge flipped off the road and left a blank spot in the landscape, abandoning the now lonely Carmen's Cafe and 4th street.

It was removed from service to be seismically retrofitted and reconstructed to accommodate the new T-3rd Street trolley line. It was placed back in service in 2006.

Once, it was manned and regularly occupied by an operator in the little window-enclosed bridge house, but not now . . . if you want to get in or out, you gotta call 'em with an hour's notice whenever you need to get a rise out of it.

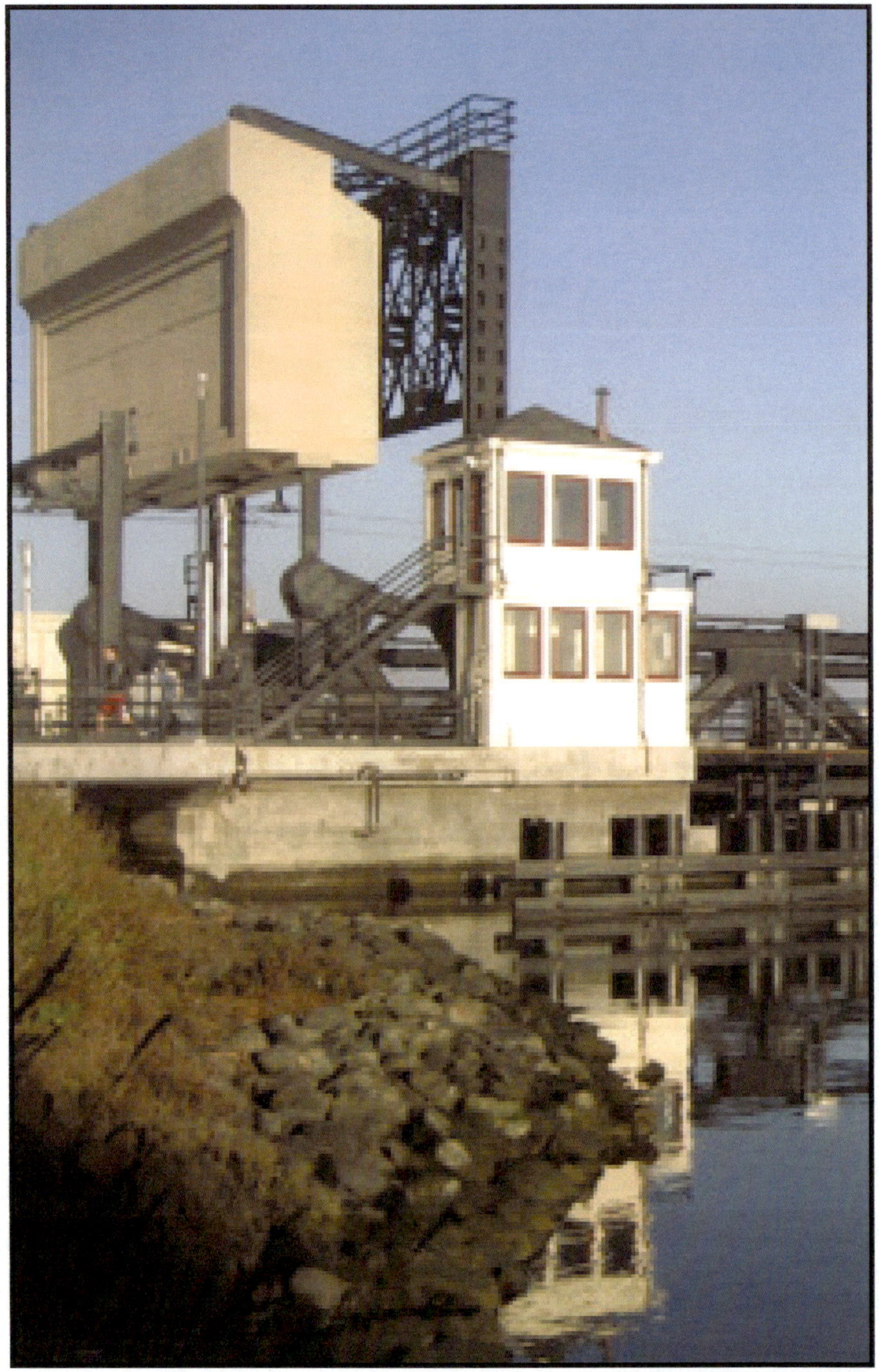

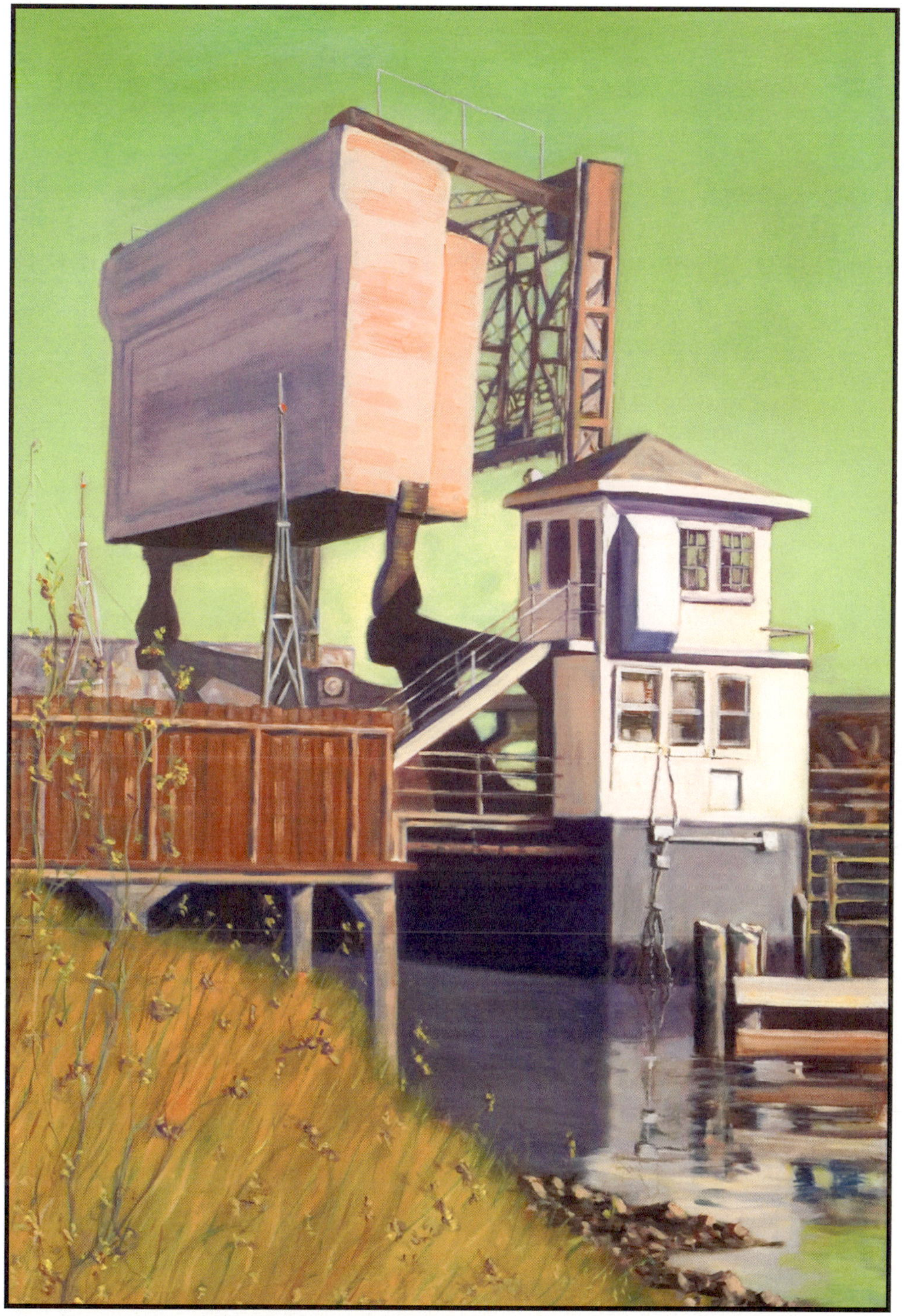

4th STREET BRIDGE Oil on Canvas 2′x 3′

NORTH BEACH POWER

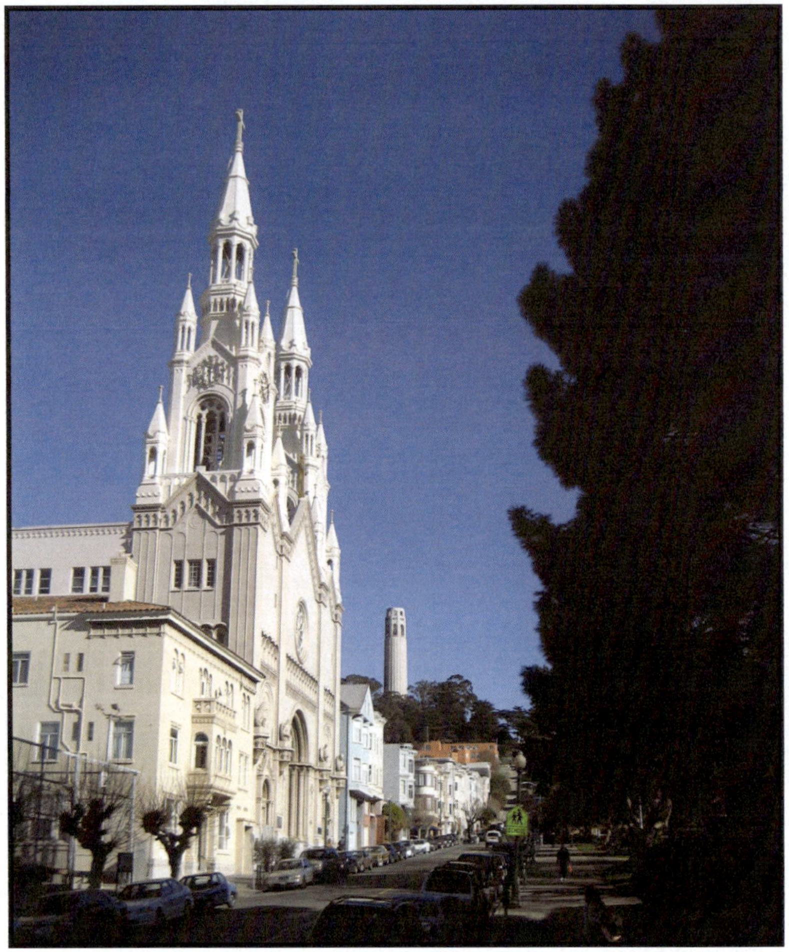

"Power to the Steeple"

Everyone knows North Beach has exerted a powerful influence worldwide as the birthplace of the Beatniks, the launching pad of the topless dancers, and the source of the new revolution of countercultural movements.

With a favorable Mediterranean climate, it has a strong ethnic Italian identity with locally owned restaurants, espresso Java cafés, boutiques and bars. When Italy is in the Wold Cup, the streets close in celebration of Italian soccer champions and victories.

It's no place for big business and shuts out any onslaught of corporate retail chain invasions, thus earning the title as one of the best neighborhoods in the country. As I see it, North Beach is the artistic heart of San Francisco, steeped in its prolonged passions.

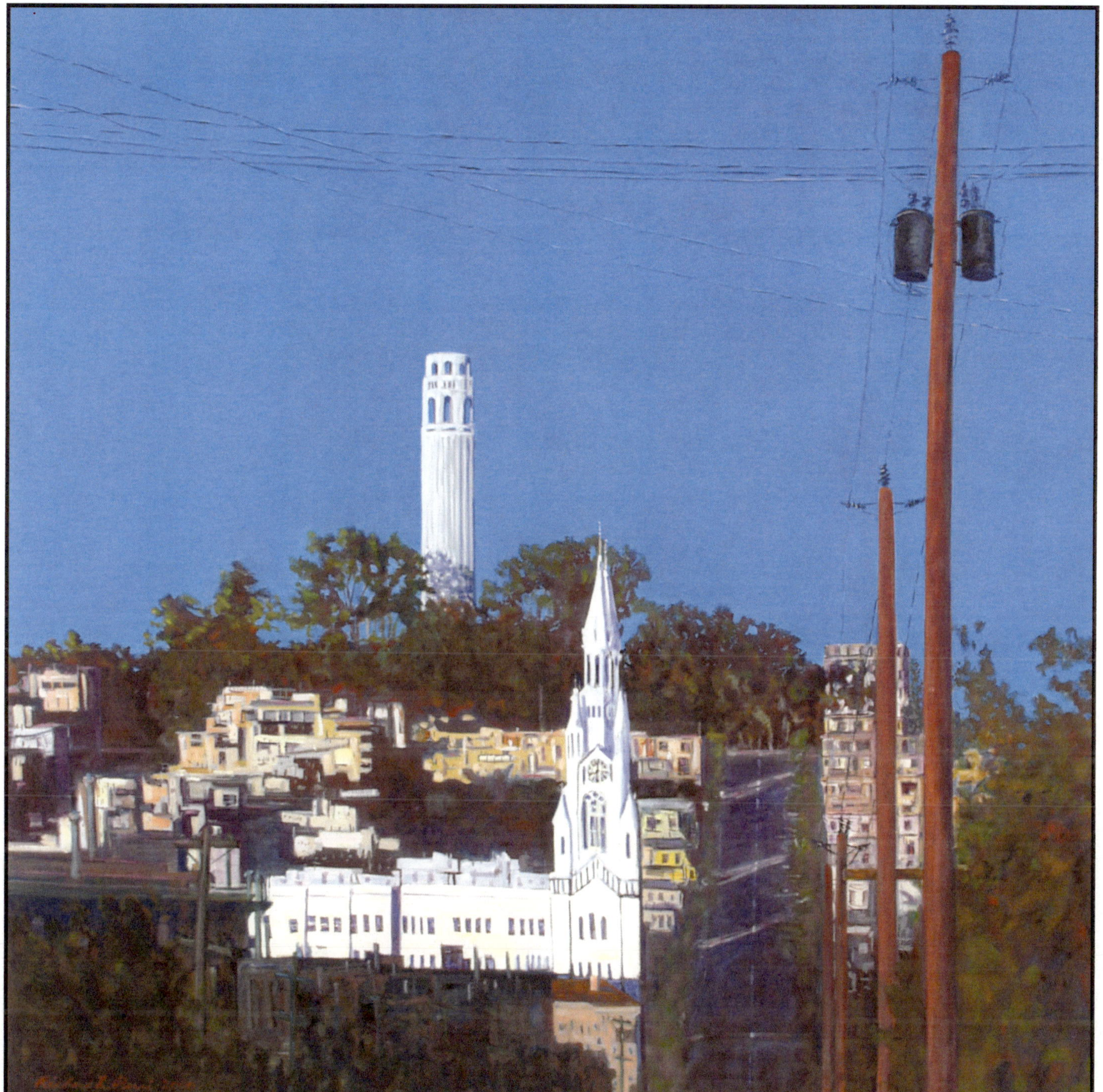

NORTH BEACH POWER Oil on Canvas 40″x 40″

ROLLING MEMORIES

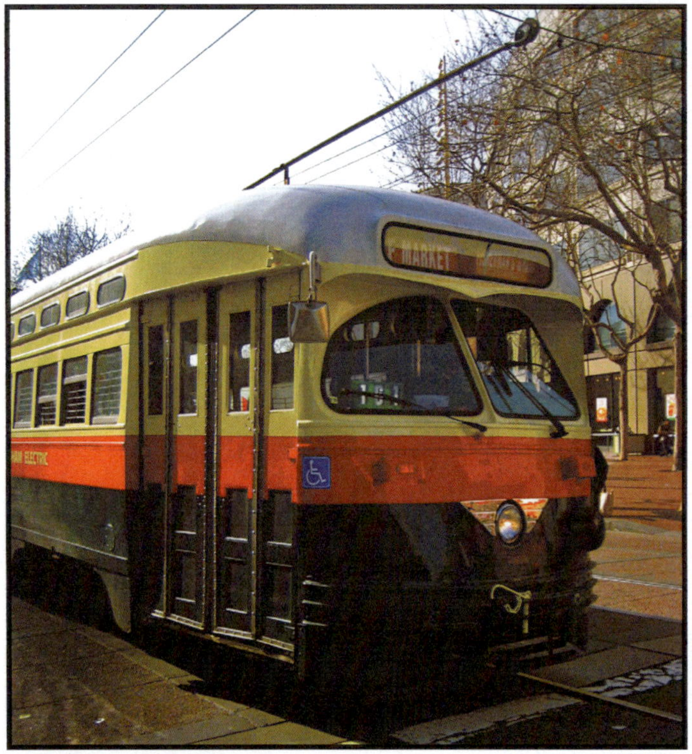

"Roll 'm in, move 'm out . . ."

With kids stealing rides by hanging on their backs, there was a time when these smiling, streamlined, ten-ton cast iron caterpillars nibbled their way across town along silver rails that strapped the city from bay to breakers.

While workers in white, blue and pink collars shared the comfortable cushioned seats of these lumbering loads, the conductor would roll through the city's congested corridors warning wayward traffic to move out of their way with the sonorous, clanging sounds of his bell.

These tireless iron transporters rolled along endlessly, day and night, rocking the city with the lullaby of their rumbling resonance. Rain or shine these rambling rollers would light up the city streets with their sparkling electrical connections.

Then the day arrived when these beloved behemoths of transit became history, replaced by imported modern metal boxes hissing along on iron wheels. Rejected and abandoned, the poor old rolling relics were cast away to South of Market bayside graveyards left to rust, ruin and decay.

Time passed and they sat still, housing homeless hoards of bums and junkies. But at last, when the retro-revivalists discovered these forlorn rollers, a rebirth rallied and the renaissance began. Old trolley operators and new train lovers, with wrench and paintbrush in hand, recalled and rebuilt the forgotten rail warriors.

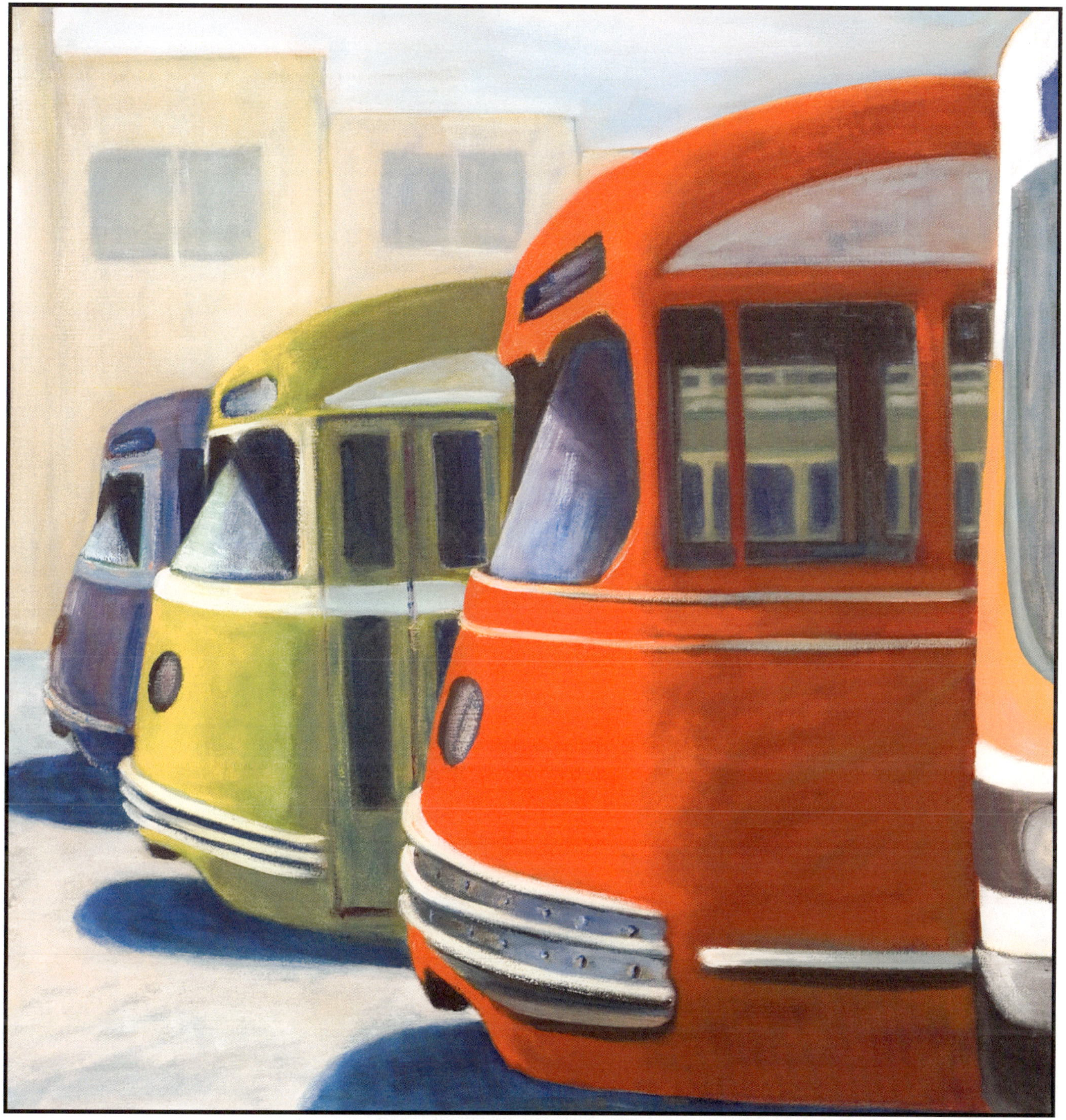

ROLLING MEMORIES Oil on Canvas 26" x 27"

EPILOGUE

Well, it was too good to last, and it didn't. You might date the end of the old watefront with the 1989 Loma Prieta earthquake, when the old Embarcadero Freeway, which was ugly as sin, was torn down.

Suddenly, the waterfront and all its denizens—the dives, the flop house hotels, the bars, were out in the sunlight, blinking in a new day.

They built a beautiful ball park on King Street, not far from Bouncers, a bar so tough that even bad guys were afraid to rob it. The customers would beat them up. Who needed cops?

One by one, the denizens of places like Red's Java House and other waterfront joints were replaced by patrons who wore designer jeans instead of Frisko jeans. A lot of the old coffee joints closed up. The ones that remained became remnants of their former self.

The waterfront is much better looking these days, much safer, much different. And much has been lost.

— Carl Nolte
San Francisco Chronicle Staff Writer

NUMINOSITY

www.ingramcontent.com/pod-product-compliance
Ingram Content Group UK Ltd.
Pitfield, Milton Keynes, MK11 3LW, UK
UKRC031203030826
14089UKWH00031B/247

* 9 7 8 1 5 8 7 9 0 4 3 3 2 *